mostly martha

A GUIDE TO FINDING BALANCE BETWEEN MARTHA AND MARY

Lanette Kinsey

mostly martha

A GUIDE TO FINDING BALANCE BETWEEN MARTHA AND MARY

WORD AFLAME PRESS

MOSTLY MARTHA

by Lanette Kinsey

© 2006 Word Aflame Press
Hazelwood MO 63042-2299
Cover design and layout by Shane Long

Scripture quotations marked "NIV" are taken from the NEW INTERNA-TIONAL VERSION®. Copyright © 1973, 1978, 1984 International Bible Society. Used by permission of Zondervan. All rights reserved. All other Scriptures are taken from the King James Version of the Bible.

Printed in the United States of America

WORD AFLAME PRESS
8855 Dunn Road, Hazelwood, MO 63042
www.pentecostalpublishing.com

Library of Congress Cataloging-in-Publication Data

Kinsey, Lanette, 1955-
    Mostly Martha / by Lanette Kinsey.
        p. cm.
    ISBN-13: 978-1-56722-696-6
    1. Christian women—Religious life. 2. Self-acceptance in women—Religious aspects—Christianity. 3. Martha, Saint. I. Title.
BV4527.K477 2006
248.8'43—dc22   2006020348
                                              CIP

For Brian, the truest Christian I know,
who with his gentleness and patience
has made all the difference in my life.

And for Lisa, Dana, and Lee,
who put up with their Martha mom
and love her anyway.

Contents

Mostly Martha

They preach and sing of Mary serving God with all her heart,
how she gave her all to you, Lord, and chose the better part.
I've journeyed through my life with its disappointments and thrills;
I've traversed many a valley and approached many a hill
to find . . . that I am mostly Martha.

I want to sit at your feet, listening so intently
that the world fades away,
But the voices of those who need me have so very much to say.
Runny noses, sticky kisses, dust and laundry, dirty dishes,
sheets to change, shirts to iron,
while trying to cook something delicious
because . . . I am mostly Martha.

I truly believe in the resurrection, in miracles and healing;
I know too well I need to spend much more time in kneeling,
and yet I have a distinct feeling
You accept my prayers while I dust:
"Keep the kids, bless this home, heal Sister Such and Such."

I so want to be like Mary, sitting at your feet,
but work and bills and children call;
they're writing with crayon on the wall!
There's a funeral tomorrow, the evangelist arrives today,
the nursery attendant quit, and help is not on the way.

Yet help me make our special times not so few and far between.
Mary moments are what I need so my soul won't get too lean.
For in communion with you I will find
peace and safety and strength of mind.
Oh, I want to be like Mary, sitting at your feet.
In my heart that's where I am.

Love,
Mostly Martha Me

Lanette Kinsey

Introduction

One of the greatest discoveries of my Christian walk is that it is okay to be real. In fact, the real you is who God wants to commune with. Yet the culture of our world persuades many of us that we are inadequate. Masks are encouraged, deceit applauded, and artifice is considered the acceptable way to get ahead. We can get so accustomed to wearing our masks in an effort to convince those around us that we are perfect and have it all together all the time that we forget to take them off even when communing with God. You may not think it possible to wear a mask before God, but it can easily be done. With trite prayers and going through the motions of praise without a true spirit of worship, we harden the mask.

The frantic pace of our world calls us to join the quest for outward perfection, all the while neglecting the heart. Only appearance matters. What lies beneath is irrelevant. Hollywood fuels the flame with its quest for eternal youth and unfading beauty. Plastered on the front of every magazine are the "beautiful" people, often strung out on drugs, dependent on pills or alcohol, with a trail of broken relationships and shattered lives behind them, yet they are applauded and lionized by society. Integrity seems outdated and irrelevant.

Frantically, they follow each other over the cliff of expectation—doing what everyone else does in order to fit in.

Only with true honesty and a spirit of submission to God can we escape the trap of trying to squeeze into self-perceived molds in an effort to please others in our social and religious circles. In any organization there is pressure to be a certain way. Whether it is a religious organization, workplace, or social organization, groups develop their own rules, ways of dress, and behavior. Group dynamics come into play, and this is actually a positive thing in many ways because it brings order and security to the group.

> *Two are better than one; because they have a good reward for their labour. For if they fall, the one will lift up his fellow: but woe to him that is alone when he falleth; for he hath not another to help him up* (Ecclesiastes 4:9, 10).

Obviously, a group can accomplish much more by combining resources. Organization is necessary to maximize the impact of those resources. The danger comes to a Christian when she finds herself striving only to meet the expectation of the group and not truly serving God.

Group rules are seldom written and rarely even acknowledged. We learn what is acceptable by observing those around us. We also strive to meet the expectations expressed in the sermons we hear and lessons that are taught, and this is wonderful as long as we do it unto the Lord and it does not become a mechanical exercise done in an effort to impress those around us.

It takes courage and a special awareness of your identity in God to face yourself head-on and assess whether your beliefs are heartfelt or whether you are just going through the motions because it is expected of you. True peace is only found in realizing that God knows exactly who you are and loves you anyway. It has been a long journey for me, from covering everything with a mask of perfection to realizing I am much more like Martha than Mary. Being honest before God has given me a greater hunger to seek more Mary attributes in my life. Of course, all Christian women are a mixture of both Mary and Martha. What we strive for is the proper balance between the two. I am still striving. I suppose I always will. But I take comfort in the verse of Scripture that says, "Now Jesus loved Martha, and her sister, and Lazarus" (John 11:5).

God Doesn't Call the Equipped

CHAPTER 1

I don't know who first said it but it is a great truth nonetheless, "God doesn't call the equipped; He equips the called." Rarely in Scripture do we find anyone who felt equipped for the task God gave him. Though Moses was reared in the royal court, he did not feel comfortable speaking to Pharaoh. Yet later, after being equipped with the staff, it seems he was never at a loss for words. Gideon, the intimidated, rose to the challenge once God equipped him with the plan for defeating the Midianites. Mary, the mother of Jesus, was called to a task for which she was certainly not equipped: to bring the Messiah into the world. Jesus chose twelve unremarkable men to spread the gospel. I doubt even one of them had an inkling where the call would take him. Certainly none seemed equipped at the time of the call for the great things he would do. It would have seemed inconceivable to Peter, Andrew, and Thomas that they would become the instruments by which the whole world would receive the gospel.

Yet we are constantly surprised at those whom

God calls. I am still surprised that He called a little girl born in the depths of bayou country in Louisiana, and definitely not equipped for the ministry. I distinctly remember being dedicated to the Lord when I was about six years old. I remember the pastor saying, "God has His hand on this little girl." Unfortunately, neither my parents nor I knew how to nurture the call, so the path through childhood and adolescence was bumpy and the call was forgotten.

I am the first-born of Leroy and Jeanie Droddy, the eldest child of a family that would grow to include five sons and two daughters. The lives of the Droddy family changed drastically when I was eleven years old. My father, who was in the oil business, moved the family to Australia. What a culture shock! We were reassured that the Australians speak English, but once we arrived we could barely understand a word. To make matters worse, they had different names for some things. A cookie was called a biscuit. What we call a biscuit is a scone. No one said, "Would you like a piece of candy?" but rather, "Have a lolly?"

We found that those who speak the "Queen's English" will ask for your Christian name when asking your first name. This is derived from the ancient custom in feudal England of naming a child after one of the saints. Your last name was called your surname, because you naturally took on the name of your father. We stumbled along and managed to pick up the fact that when people asked for your surname, they wanted to know your last name, but we never heard the term, "Christian name."

Five months after our arrival my mom went to the hospital for the delivery of her sixth child. When she checked in, the nurse taking her information asked for her surname.

"Droddy," she said. "D-r-o-d-d-y."

"Yes, madam, and your Christian name?" the nurse enquired.

"United Pentecostal," Mom replied proudly. "U-n-i-t-e-d P-e-n-t-e-c-o-s-t-a-l."

Whereupon the nurse replied, "My, what an unusual name."

By then the light was dawning upon my parents, but Mom was too embarrassed to correct it. We laugh about this today, wondering if Tommy is still on the records in Australia as the son of Mrs. United Pentecostal Droddy.

Our house was always full of people and animals, which could be the reason my own poor, deprived children have never had a pet. I have been bitten on the toes by my brothers' hamsters in the middle of the night, traumatized by a cat who insisted on bringing mouse heads to my mother, and butted by a pet goat. We owned a parrot that could spit seed husks for yards and screeched "Hello" for thirty minutes each time the telephone rang. Then there was a succession of dogs, one of which was certifiably retarded. He would howl as if he were in mortal pain every time a car horn sounded. Naturally, my brothers thought that was hilarious, so they would blow the horn just to laugh at the tortured animal. Of course, there were the inevitable deaths and pet funerals, and then I would be surrounded by sniffling, brokenhearted siblings.

Not only did my parents let the boys bring stray animals home; from time to time we also took in stray people. Anyone hungry, lonely, or in need could find a good meal at our house. To my mom, already cooking for nine people, an extra two, three, or four (or twenty) did not make that much difference. Our kitchen was always open, and as long as someone needed to eat, Mom would cook. Although she never said so, I am pretty sure Mom went hungry a few times in her childhood. Abandoned by her mother at five months of age and raised by an alcoholic father, she must have lived through times there was not enough to eat. So it is understandable that she finds immense satisfaction in feeding others. It is not the food itself that she loves. She is petite, and getting her to sit down and actually eat for her own sake is next to impossible. The serving is what she loves. Seeing someone hungry or having to do without basic necessities will get her ire up faster than anything. My quiet and longsuffering dad never complained. God blessed him in his career so that he was able to provide the means to feed all those people. There was always someone coming or going, and he took it in stride.

The home of Martha, Mary, and Lazarus seems much the same. It was the center for hospitality. Jesus and His disciples knew this house would always have a meal and a place to refresh themselves. These hospitality stations don't appear by themselves. They take hard work and organization. They require a Martha.

We returned to the United States in early 1975, and I experienced culture shock all over again. While embracing the doctrine of Oneness and speaking in tongues as the initial evidence of receiving the gift of the Holy Ghost, the Australian church was very different in custom, practice, and worship. Getting used to the American church and deciding on my career path produced confusion in my spirit. Then God sent a lifeline in the form of Brian Kinsey. Marriage was definitely not on my mind when I stepped into a small country church outside New Orleans on a Sunday night. I did not know until much later that Brian, the evangelist for the evening, leaned over and said to the assistant pastor, "I'm going to marry that girl." It seemed like a chance encounter, yet today, thirty years later, I see the hand of God all over it. I had forgotten the words of the pastor at my dedication, but God never forgets His promises. You would have to look hard to find a less equipped person to be a minister's wife than me, yet, seven months later, that is exactly what I became.

Instant Evangelist's Wife

CHAPTER 2

Brian and I got married on a Saturday afternoon and started our first revival together the following Wednesday. He had been evangelizing for almost a year when we married, and though he had stayed busy, our future was far from assured. Our honeymoon consisted of driving through several states to get to our first revival as husband and wife, and when we rolled into town on that Wednesday afternoon, I was terrified. I knew I was in no way equipped to be the evangelist's wife. I felt very intimidated but I soon had other things to think about.

We had been married for only four days. The church was small, with no evangelist's quarters, and I suppose the pastor's family did not have room for us, for they put us in the home of the assistant pastor and his wife, which was nice and clean but had only one bedroom. But that would be okay, they explained, because the assistant pastor worked nights. We would have the bed at night, while his wife slept on the couch, and he would have it during the day. Welcome to the evangelistic field! Married four days and sharing a bed with the assistant pastor. Since I had not thought to pack a set of queen size sheets for our exclusive use and we certainly did not have enough money to purchase any, we had no choice in the matter.

We ended up having a decent revival although I remember little about it except those sheets. To be honest, where we slept was the least of my worries. What *really* worried me was measuring up to the expectations of others. I knew it was very important to look the part, so I made sure to dress right and fix my hair to look "Pentecostal." I began a quest to become the perfect preacher's wife.

From the vantage point of age and experience, I now understand my priorities were wrong. My heart was in the right place—I sincerely loved God and wanted to do His work—but I tried hard to do it all myself. The Scripture says, "Seek ye first the kingdom of God, and his righteousness; and all these things shall be added unto you" (Matthew 6:33). "Things," of course, refers to clothing, food, (where you will sleep), and the less important details of life. Though not consciously, I sought to get the outer package just right without seeking the kingdom of God in the depths that I should. This can be the mark of an immature Christian, for I see it in young women all the time—and sadly, in many older women also—the outer package seems perfect, but there is nothing inside. As the old cliché goes, "The light is on, but no one is home." Instead of seeking the kingdom of God first, they have sought the "right look" or appearance that all is well while neglecting the inner self.

This is not to say that the outer package is not important. Industry spends billions of dollars each year on packaging because people tend to buy the product in the fancy package before the one in the plain package. Furthermore, what is on the outside of the package is expected to be a fair representation of what is on the inside. We expect French cut green beans to be inside if there is a picture of them on the outside. That is why Christian women should not buy into the argument that only what is inside is important. People often quote "The LORD looketh on the heart," but leave out the significance of the previous statement, "for man looketh on the outward appearance" (I Samuel 16:7). If the world cannot tell we are different by looking at our outward package, they will have less incentive to explore the inner contents.

Observing a person in many situations is required to make a judgment about what dwells within, but those around us should be able to tell at a glance that an Apostolic woman is different. Recently, while I was unloading groceries from the cart into my car, a young man walked by me, cursing a blue streak. As he glanced at me he did a double take and said, "Excuse me, ma'am, I didn't mean anything." I was not the only woman unloading groceries in the parking lot, but I was the only one who received an apology. I believe it is because I looked like a lady, a person whom someone should not curse around.

While we certainly cannot tell the state of a person's heart by their outward appearance, you can be assured that our appearance goes a long way in affecting how we are treated. Our youngest daughter, Dana, was told of a conversation between two professors at the college she attended while pursuing a degree in elementary education. One was telling the other of his concern at discussing the content that would have to be covered in an upcoming class discussion in front of Miss Kinsey. Dana had never spoken with either of these professors about her religious convictions or family background. All she did was show up in class with beautiful, uncut hair and modest clothing, and that spoke volumes. Her outer packaging said, "I am not cheap or vulgar. I am a lady."

People are looking at the outside. They do not have x-ray vision or God vision. They only see the outward package. If the package is dressed like a tramp, spectators will expect the same to be inside. Obviously, we are not discussing groceries, so it must be understood that in people, what is on the outside is not always a representation of what is on the inside. Many women simply dress provocatively because they have never been taught and do not understand the protective power of modesty. But women who wonder why they are treated less than respectfully in public should consider the packaging. A walk through any mall in America is a sobering experience as we watch the parade of prepubescent and adolescent girls who are not being taught this. It is no wonder they are treated as sex objects by the boys in their lives. Their clothing is screaming, "Take me. I'm cheap." They do not understand the power of packaging.

Though it is human nature to make judgments

about people based on their outward appearance, we must never forget that beneath a provocative or tough exterior can lie a heart that is longing for God. A few years ago a beautiful, six-foot tall, young lady walked into my office. She had numerous tattoos and multiple piercings. She and her boyfriend had just received the Holy Ghost and realized their need to get married. I agreed to make her a dress suitable for the wedding, all the while thinking, "There is no way this girl is going to make it. She doesn't have a clue." But I was dead wrong. As the days went by she shed her worldly trappings one by one until a few weeks later she walked up to me after service and asked me to hold out my hand, whereupon she deposited the last holdout: her tongue stud. After I got over the "yuck" factor, I had to chuckle and remind myself all over again that God looks on the heart. Beneath that tough, tattooed and pierced body was a hunger for something to fill the empty place that had always been in her heart. All she needed was someone to introduce her to the Master.

Though we should never buy into the argument that the outward appearance is not important, we should also never forget that God is looking at our heart. For the churched, it is very easy to focus on getting the outward appearance just right because we know everyone is looking, but without an inward cleansing all the outward perfection in the world will not bring inner peace.

I tried to find peace by having an extremely ordered world. Some of this is personality based but taken to the extreme can drive everyone crazy. Like

Martha, I wanted everything perfect. I worked hard for the perfect marriage, perfect grooming, perfect housekeeping, the perfect kids, with perfect manners and perfect grades. Then life happened! And I found out there was no possible way to keep everything perfect all the time. That is when a Martha can give in to despair and only a Mary solution can help. Worship is the key. We must get to the place where the search for personal perfection fades against feeding the inner man at the feet of Jesus Christ.

A frantic quest for personal perfection can easily lead to burnout, which occurs when you rely only on the fuel you produce through your good works. If you are talented or very structured you can keep going for some time. However, that fuel source will eventually run dry. A woman experiencing burnout will often say, "I feel like I am just going through the motions." And, believe it or not, there is something to be said for going through the motions. The good thing is that everything looks right and you probably will not be challenged by those who do not know you very well. Mechanically going through the motions will keep you doing all the things you should, in all the ways you should, for a long time. But the bad thing about going through the motions is you will eventually burn out because your actions are not being fed by inner passion. Inner passion can only be found at the feet of Jesus. Worshiping the Master will replenish your spirit like nothing else can.

The best solution is to never reach the burnout phase, but if you do, don't despair. Just get to the feet of

Jesus. There you can reorder your priorities through worship. As the old song says, once you turn your eyes toward Jesus, the things of earth will grow strangely dim in the light of His glory and grace.[1] At His feet you can plug into an energy source that will never fade, flicker, or run dry. Temporal things will retreat in importance and what really matters will come into view.

> *Therefore we do not lose heart. Though outwardly we are wasting away, yet inwardly we are being renewed day by day. For our light and momentary troubles are achieving for us an eternal glory that far outweighs them all. So we fix our eyes not on what is seen, but on what is unseen. For what is seen is temporary, but what is unseen is eternal. Now we know that if the earthly tent we live in is destroyed, we have a building from God, an eternal house in heaven, not built by human hands. Meanwhile we groan, longing to be clothed with our heavenly dwelling* (II Corinthians 4:16-5:2, NIV).

Mostly Martha

CHAPTER 3

For many years I sat on a pew, silently identifying with Martha. Because of my upbringing and nature, I could visualize her dilemma perfectly. I did not verbalize my feelings however, because all the sermons seemed to be about Mary, sitting at the feet of Jesus, and I certainly did not want anyone thinking I was less than spiritual! But I have always suspected that if I had been in the household of Martha, Mary, and Lazarus, I would have been the one in the kitchen complaining and muttering about Mary not realizing how much needed to be done, and feeling like a martyr.

As Jesus and his disciples were on their way, he came to a village where a woman named Martha opened her home to him. She had a sister called Mary, who sat at the Lord's feet listening to what he said. But Martha was distracted by all the preparations that had to be made. She came to him and asked, "Lord, don't you care that my sister has left me to do the work by myself? Tell her to help me!" "Martha, Martha," the Lord answered, "you are worried and upset about many things, but only one thing is needed. Mary has chosen what is better, and it will not be taken away from her" (Luke 10:38-42, NIV).

Ouch! Poor Martha—the only woman recorded in the New Testament to receive a rebuke from the lips of Jesus Christ. You never hear sermons about what a great person Martha was. No one encourages you to be Martha. In fact, she gets a pretty bad rap most of the time. Mary is who we all strive to be, with good cause. Jesus said she chose the better part, and who does not want to be commended by Jesus?

Although I am sure Martha and Mary lived very full lives, it seems obvious that the demands upon women have changed drastically since the days when Jesus walked the earth. If Martha had trouble then, imagine if she had lived in the twenty-first century as a woman expected to find the time to sit at the feet of Jesus while being a wife, mother, cook, nurse, bookkeeper, referee, tutor, and all the other things required to run a modern household. Whether in ancient times or now, women know and bear the burden of the expectations of the people in their lives. They understand the needs of their husbands and families, often before they know themselves, and this leads to a dilemma that the title of Cathy Lechner's book describes in a nutshell, *I'm Trying to Sit at His Feet but Who's Going to Cook Dinner?* We would *LOVE* to sit at the feet of Jesus. In fact, we would love to sit anywhere! The average woman of today's generation is stretched so thin that sitting is hardly an option for any reason.

Although I know my minister husband loves my Mary qualities, when he comes home at the end of a long day, he is looking for Martha. He needs a clean home, a nice dinner (or at least a plan to get some dinner) and a place to relax. When my children were small and got home from school they wanted a Martha mom, with snacks at the ready. If Martha had not been in the kitchen preparing the food when Jesus and the disciples visited, guess what the disciples would have said about fifteen minutes after their arrival?

"Uh, Sister Martha, when is dinner?"

It seems apparent that Jesus and His entourage visited the home of Martha, Mary, and Lazarus often and knew what to expect. They knew they could rely on Martha for a good meal and shelter for the night. It is thought that Martha was the older sister, possibly a widow, since the house is referred to as hers. If that was true, it would be natural for her to be in charge and even to be anxious about the hospitality. As an older sister, I can relate to her feelings of frustration. Older sisters tend to feel the weight of the world on their shoulders. They feel responsible for seeing that all goes right in a family.

My only sister, Jeanie, is nine years, three months, and twelve days younger than I. (The age gap is a running joke with us. She loves to rub it in by saying that I am ten years older than she, while I say I am nine years older.) Although I remember being thrilled when a little sister was born, as we got older it seemed I was usually in the house assisting my mother in cooking and cleaning, while Jeanie basically lived outside with our five brothers or with her friends. I remember being anxious over my brothers many times, while Jeanie did not seem to have a care in the world. If the boys did not show up at home on time or if their grades were suffering, I worried. No one expected it of me. Worry over my siblings was a self-imposed burden—just because I'm a big sister.

As women take on the roles of wife and mother they find more reasons than ever to be a Martha. The preacher's wife (particularly the pastor's wife) is usually *required* to be a Martha. She is expected to be a perfect hostess, wife, and mother; run the ladies' auxiliary, music, and special programs; provide counseling and comfort; look like a million dollars, even when she's buying groceries; never be grouchy or touchy; and always be available as the helpmeet of her husband, to compliment and support his sermons, and run interference for him from the church busybody. But she is also expected to be like Mary. Obviously, she must be the most spiritual woman in the church, lead ladies' prayer, always be in the prayer room, and worship the most.

You do not have to be a minister's wife, however, to experience and understand the internal struggle between the Martha nature and the Mary nature in each of us. All women are a combination of the two, with a tendency toward one or the other. When Martha becomes dominant we tend to fuss a lot and worry over petty things that (as the old timers used to say) "don't amount to a hill of beans." When Mary is dominant, dishes can pile up around her ears and she really does not seem to notice. All that matters is communion with God. The "perfect" woman would be the right balance of the two natures. However, when you meet the perfect woman, please let me know. She is about as rare as the perfect man, and I am pretty sure he is extinct.

Women are exceedingly complex creatures, a fact of which our husbands are well aware. We have all heard the joke about God creating Adam, then deciding he could improve on that, whereupon He made woman. Although I would not go so far as to say God *improved* His creation, He certainly added a dimension to the emotional makeup of females not found in males.

Women tend to be emotion driven, while men are usually maddeningly logical. A man cannot possibly understand how a woman's emotions can change her thinking from one minute to the next. It is unfathomable to him that what is perfectly acceptable one day can be completely unacceptable the next. And heaven help the poor man who dares to challenge this change in acceptability status!

We could speculate that the complex nature of women is reflected in the household of Martha, Mary, and Lazarus. It takes two women to represent the dual nature of the female, while the male requires only one person. Where could we go with that one, ladies? Nowhere in the Scriptures is there a dual example for the perfect man like the Mary/Martha example. Peter was simply Peter, the rock. Highly volatile, passionate about whatever he did. Paul, the apostle, was always the same—orator, scholar, teacher.

If we accept the household of Martha as representative of the male and female natures, we could say men are simple minded and they could say women have split personalities. All joking aside, we realize that men are complex creations of God. It would be simplistic to say that all men are one way or another; however, most psychologists agree that the thought processes of men and women are very different.

Many Christian women deal with guilt because they cannot be perfect in every way, and many men have a hard time understanding that facet of the female psyche. Women can easily forget they are only human and accept the fallacy that they have to do everything right all the time. A good mental picture of the Christian woman's daily walk is to imagine yourself on a tightrope. Lions of the world are one side, ready to tear your children and family values to shreds. On the other side is Niagara Falls, the daily tasks that are never quite done and can so easily wash you into a sweeping tide of distraction. It is hard enough to keep your balance on the tightrope, but compounding the task are your perceptions of the expectations of others. So often, rather than focusing on pleasing God, we focus on externals that do not matter. Trivial things become giants that want to knock us off balance. Suddenly, we can find ourselves hanging off the end of the proverbial rope, holding frantically to the very last knot we have tied in it, wondering, "What happened?" One day I was serving God and today I have been blindsided by life. Yesterday I was Mary and today I am all Martha. We have lost focus of the reason we are on the journey and we have lost our joy.

We need balance to be able to walk the tightrope of life with the joy and peace of God, devoid of fear, with the assurance that God knows exactly who and what we are. He knows our strengths and weaknesses. As long as Martha insists on organizing everything and being in control, the Lord will let her. When we surrender and let Mary rise in worship, fear and tension fade. Only intimate fellowship with the Master will free us from leaning on our own resources. Only when we put our total trust in Him and let Him be in charge can we relax and reclaim our joy.

Feeding Mary

CHAPTER 4

Mary and Martha personify the two facets of most women. The Martha side is typified in the practical, busy, get everything done aspect of our personality, while Mary represents the spiritual side of our nature—the part of us that longs to soak in the good things of God. We know we ought to be more like Mary, yet the Martha side often takes over because we live in the real world. Women are explicitly commanded by the apostle Paul to be keepers of their homes (Titus 2:5). Though the world has changed drastically since Paul's day, we are still required to keep our homes and families together in the face of unprecedented pressure.

There are few things that challenge the balance of consecration and duty as much as motherhood. As the mother of three children I fully understand morning chaos. I also understand and have heard it taught many times that the best way to start your day is with Jesus. It has proven true in my life that the way to feed the Mary part of me is with a personal, daily devotion.

My voice shalt thou hear in the morning, O LORD; in the morning will I direct my prayer unto thee, and will look up (Psalm 5:3).

Cause me to hear thy lovingkindness in the morning; for in thee do I trust: cause me to know the way wherein I should walk; for I lift up my soul unto thee (Psalm 143:8).

If we can manage our daily devotion in the morning, things go better for the rest of the day. It causes us to know where and how we should walk that day and sets the tone for interaction with people we will meet. An ideal day is one where Mom can get up early and commune with the Lord over coffee or tea while the rest of the household is asleep. Or, if she is not an early riser, she gets everyone out the door for the day and then does her devotion.

But sometimes, things just don't work out as we planned. Getting up and down with a sick child all night can really put a crimp in your style. The alarm clock that does not go off, necessitating a mad rush for the bus, can throw off the rhythm of the whole day. When you finally get the kids out the door, the phone rings. You have a doctor's appointment, laundry to do, clothes to iron, bathrooms to clean, and groceries to buy. Before you know it, the kids are coming in the door from school and the mad dash begins to cook dinner while helping with homework, feed everyone when Dad gets home, clean the kitchen, bathe kids, put them to bed, and then start all over again. You have helped the children say their prayers, but you fall into bed, too exhausted to do much more than say, "Thank you Lord for this day. I'll do better tomorrow. Amen."

Most women have to add a full-time job to this mix, not to mention the extra activities in which a busy family is involved—regular church attendance, music lessons, soccer practice—the list goes on. The lady of the house often takes care of the finances and is almost always the coordinator of family activities. She is expected to know where all stray socks and shoes can be found, monitor and arbitrate all disputes, be a loving wife to her husband, and still find time to sit at the feet of Jesus, which she would have to get up at 4:00 AM to do. Unless you are one of those chirpy morning people (an abomination to we night people) you are not going to be very good company at 4:00 AM.

This can be quite a dilemma because then we feel guilty for not being the superwoman who can get everything done and still get up at the crack of dawn for devotion time. Guilt can lead to depression and depression can lead to resentment and resentment can lead to anger. You can begin a cycle of self-destruction, where you just give up because you cannot reach the expectation you have set for yourself. It is vital to grasp the fact that God understands the seasons of our lives.

> *Like as a father pitieth his children, so the LORD pitieth them that fear him. For he knoweth our frame; he remembereth that we are dust. As for man, his days are as grass: as a flower of the*

field, so he flourisheth. For the wind passeth over it, and it is gone; and the place thereof shall know it no more. But the mercy of the LORD is from everlasting to everlasting upon them that fear him, and his righteousness unto children's children (Psalm 103:13-17).

God knows our frame. He knows we are dust, because He made us. He knows as long as we live in our own mortal bodies, we will fail from time to time. That is why the Scripture reassures us that the mercy of the Lord is from everlasting to everlasting. There is not a single instance of Jesus rejecting anyone who threw herself on His mercy. Of course that does not give us license to take His mercy for granted but it does give us strength to get up and try again. If we had a friend who constantly wronged us, we would find it audacious for her to repeat the same offense over and over again and expect to be forgiven each time. Jesus' love for us, however, is not based on the premise that we will never fail or on how many times we have been forgiven. His love reaches for us constantly. His mercy has nothing to do with our goodness but, like any friend, we need regular communication to stay close. The better the communication the more intimate our relationship will become.

I was blessed to hear Thetus Tenney speak about seasons of life when I was a very young mother, with two small daughters and a son who would come along the following year, just at the time we began pastoring a church. How often her wise words comforted my guilty heart when it seemed I just could not do it all. "It" being meeting the expectations of other people who seemed to expect the preacher's wife to be at the side of her husband at every camp meeting, conference, home Bible study, counseling session, and birthday party. She spoke of staying at home with her babies while her husband traveled and how she used the time after getting them to bed for studying the Word of God. This season of study sustained her through the later times when busyness took over and there was not as much time to study. She explained that we should expect there will be seasons of life, and the most important thing you can do with each one is accept it and realize that it will change. The important thing is to do your best in the season you are in.

I always knew the importance of reading the Word of God. My mother was diligent in reading a portion of Scripture each day and once had all the passengers of a trans-Pacific flight looking for a Bible so that she would not miss a day of reading. In the scramble of getting seven children to the airport, her Bible had accidentally been placed in the stowed luggage rather than the hand luggage. She was determined not to let a day go by without reading the Word and asked the flight attendants to find her a Bible. They could not find one and were just about to look in the life raft (to mollify this crazy lady) when a nun offered her prayer book, which had the Psalms in it. I am sure everyone sighed with relief—I was too busy trying to pretend I didn't know this person. Even though I found this incident highly embarrassing as a thirteen- or fourteen-year-old, it made an impact on me, and sometime later, I adopted the same principle, although I did not have a structured plan.

On New Year's Day following our wedding, Brian handed me a BREAD chart (a plan for reading the entire Bible in a year) and asked me to follow it, and I have continued a yearly reading plan since that time. I guess by then he had figured out he'd married a Martha and needed to do something about it! By the time Lee was born, the One Year Bible had been introduced, which I found easier than following a chart, although some prefer that method and enjoy checking off the days. Tackling the whole Bible can seem a daunting task but, broken into small increments, becomes manageable for even the busiest mothers. It only takes a few minutes of your day, but there is immense personal satisfaction and untold spiritual gains to be made by reading the Bible through each year. As each of our children grew and became ready to have their own personal devotion, we presented that one with a One Year Bible of his or her own to encourage a lifelong habit of Bible reading.

When your children are small you may find it hard to carve out large chunks of time for prayer, but you can talk to the Lord all through the day. Make Him a companion with whom you talk about everything. As you clean, as you cook, as you drive, He is a faithful friend who is always listening. That is the only way you can follow the admonition to "Pray without ceasing" (I Thessalonians 5:17).

As your children grow older, include them in your times of prayer. I do not recommend that you make them spend hours on their knees; however, they can join the family prayer time for at least a few minutes, depending on their age. Seeing you incorporate a lifestyle of prayer paints a powerful word picture in their minds that will never leave them. Our kids still talk about a night where we took all three of them to the church with their pillows and books and toys for an all-night family prayer meeting. We prayed together briefly and then let the children go about their business of play while we continued to pray. Lee was about three years old, and as he played, he ran headlong into the remembrance table in front of the pulpit. Instantly, a huge blue knot arose on his forehead. Brian laid his hand on his head and prayed, and almost as fast, the knot went away. Although Lee was really too young to understand, the girls have never forgotten that night. Seeing answers to even these simple prayers builds faith and provides a powerful incentive to pray the next time there is a need.

Pray together for family needs and then rejoice when those needs are met. Discuss it around your table. Pray with your children at night while tucking them into bed. Make it a habit to visit the prayer room before the church service begins. All of this will help establish a lifestyle of prayer for your children. I have known the occasional parent who tries to force her child into long, intensive times of prayer. To do this is to risk having it become a chore to be dreaded rather than a time of communion with God. Remember, their attention span is limited and boredom sets in quickly. Short, directed prayers will be much more effective in keeping them focused.

The rewards of a consistent devotion time are far

reaching. Much is accomplished personally as those small increments of time add up until the whole Bible has been read through in a year and as you grow closer to the Lord in prayer. What becomes a way of life with you naturally flows into your children, and you will be thrilled to see their own devotional lives develop. Lastly, the kingdom of God is enriched by your prayers for others.

The only way to grow the Mary side of you is to feed it the bread of life and worship at His feet. This also requires pushing back the plate occasionally in times of fasting. Joy Haney stated, "Prayer and the Word give you a certain depth in God, but fasting adds new depth because the flesh is decreased while the spirit increases."[2] Fasting adds layers of richness to your devotional life that cannot be added any other way.

Life has come full circle now. We started out without children, of course, when we could pray and read the Bible on any schedule we liked. Then we moved to the hectic house-full-of-small-children season, to the all-teenager household (where most mothers *really* learn to pray) to the children-leaving-the-nest season. Now the nicest part of the day is when everyone has gone to school or work, the house is quiet and empty, and I can make my coffee and visit with the Lord at my leisure. I must admit that I get the beds made and the kitchen clean before I begin so the Martha side of me won't come peeking out. And I often think of Thetus Tenney.

Feeding Mary

God,
bless all young mothers at end of day,
kneeling wearily with each
small one
to hear them pray.
Too tired to rise when done . . .
and yet, they do,
longing just to sleep one whole night through.
Too tired to sleep . . .
too tired to pray. . . .
God
bless all young mothers
at close of day.[3]

Ruth Bell Graham

Thwarting Martha

CHAPTER 5

You really don't have to worry too much about feeding the Martha side of your personality. Rather, we often have to squelch the Martha nature, for it comes roaring out without much provocation. Martha's biggest problem seems to be that she wanted to get everything done, in *her* time and *her* way. There is no doubt that her work was vitally important to the household. There was no doubt that people needed to be fed or that she needed help serving. Jesus did not tell Martha to stop what she was doing. He said, "You are worried and upset about many things" (Luke 10:41, NIV). He was telling her to relax and discover what was really important. Dinner could wait, but sitting at His feet would not always be possible. An overarching sense of duty can skew the priorities of a Martha in record time. We must always keep in mind that getting the job done to perfection is not nearly as important as the reason we are doing it.

Have you ever cooked a big dinner and called everyone to come eat and then got impatient with their dawdling? You can find yourself feeling persecuted because you have slaved over a hot stove for people who do not appreciate it enough to come to eat while the food is fresh and hot. It is easy to forget to be thankful that we have food to cook and a family to feed, because we are focused on the wrong things.

There are three very painful words that will help that "Martha-ness." They are: *give up control!* The compulsion toward overcontrol has probably caused more nervous breakdowns and fractured lives than any other factor in the lives of women. Invariably, at some point, there will come a situation that cannot be controlled, causing an emotional crisis. Not only is the desire to control damaging for a woman; it is also damaging to those around her. By not allowing our children to make mistakes and controlling every aspect of their lives, we can damage their self-esteem. A woman who refuses to relinquish control in family, financial, and spiritual matters to her husband will cause instability in the home.

There is no doubt that the impulse to organize everything is part of the makeup of the female psyche. God put in us a desire to nurture, and when that desire is thwarted it is easy to deteriorate into Martha Mania, where we are worried and upset about many things. This is what we must guard against. There are things that absolutely have to be done, but we must not allow the doing of it to take precedence over the important things in our lives. We have to learn to do all the things we need to do without getting overly stressed and without taking away from our time with God. Once we have calmed down it is easy to see some things are only important in our minds and the world will not fall down around our ears if they are postponed.

Mary certainly was not worried. She could have sat there all day listening to the words of Jesus. Her mind-set was, "Forget food. Forget serving. Just give me Jesus, and I will be all right." Mary knew the food was not going to vanish and when the time was right, they would eat. She had the wonderful gift of being able to set the mundane aside and focus on the moment that would not last forever. We have all had them—a sudden urge to pray, a friend in need of an encouraging word—a moment that will pass and never come again. It cannot be postponed. The time to pray is right then. The time to stop to encourage a friend is now. If we do not respond immediately, the unction fades and an oppor-tunity to make a difference in someone's life or in the kingdom of God can pass us by.

Not only does Mary know how to seize the moment—she is constantly on the lookout for an occa-sion to worship the Master. She has the gift of being able to shut out all distraction and totally immerse her-self in the presence of God. I enjoy watching the "Mostly Mary" types. There is at least one in every church. Often she is a single mom who lives in reduced circumstances. Her five or six kids, who are slightly grubby, are doing back flips over the pews while she is in the altar oblivious to everything but soaking in the grace of God. There is an old saying, "She is so heav-enly minded she's no earthly good." And yet did you notice that her kids *do* get fed, they *do* get to church, she *does* survive somehow? And she aggravates the Marthas! Because Martha wants her to pay a little more attention to the details. We are the ones tying her kids to the pews so that she can commune with God without the church coming down around her ears!

It is that pesky overcontrol problem again. Martha tends to think that everything has to be perfect before she can worship while Mary thinks nothing matters except worship. It seems quite possible to me that, taken to this extreme, both can be wrong. One who tends to be a Martha can unconsciously resent Mary for her lack of attention to detail, while Mary can despise Martha for her "carnality." Though not the primary focus of the passage of Scripture in Luke 10, which is obviously about worship, there is a secondary lesson to be learned in the Mary/Martha example: we need balance. Balance is a dirty word to both Mary and Martha because it implies lack of control, and control *is* the issue.

The need to overcontrol is rooted in a lack of faith, and both Martha and Mary can suffer from this malady. Each must learn to manage her spirit and to have faith in God. The danger in letting either quality get out of control comes when we are inevitably hit with the disappointments of life. Martha can have trouble handling tragedy because she thinks on a sub-conscious level that she is somehow exempt because she has been careful to do everything right. She has taken care that all the outward trappings are perfectly aligned, cleaned, and straightened. Mary can be blind-sided by tragedy because she really *has* put everything at the feet of Jesus in worship, yet trouble still comes. Sometimes a Mary feels she deserves more because of her devotion. Both have to learn that we can do nothing to deserve the grace of God. Neither devotion nor duty buys us a ticket out of trouble.

Balance comes when we forget ourselves and gain eternal perspective. It is really not important whether I consider myself a Mary or a Martha. The lessons of life are painful for each, and Jesus loved them both.

My Way or the Highway

CHAPTER 6

I once knew a fine, gracious lady who was very much a Martha in that she always opened her home in hospitality. She was also a Mary: devout in prayer, church attendance, and faithful to God in every way, except one. My friend, whom I will call Ann, though raised in church and at the time serving as youth director, married a man who was not a Christian. I knew her years later after she had worked hard to put her husband through medical school. By this time they had two children and Ann's husband had decided to put her aside and move in with a nurse with whom he worked. It was devastating to Ann and the children, of course. She asked the church to stand with her in believing that her husband would return to her and accept truth. Everyone rallied to her side, but as time passed, it became obvious the man had no intention of returning. She would not listen to those who gently tried to steer her toward acceptance of the breach.

Ann did everything humanly possible to please the man who had left her. All her Martha attributes were brilliantly displayed as she tried in every way to win him back. Ann's Mary attributes also intensified, with extended periods of fasting and prayer. She and the children prayed every morning and every night for Dad to come home. Almost every waking breath was devoted to discussion of God's will for families to be together. She drilled the children with verses about how God hates divorce and how every prayer we pray will be answered.

But Ann forgot one thing. She forgot to ask for God's will. She had only one right outcome in mind for her situation. This did not just go on for ten weeks or ten months, but for at least ten years. The children, who were told daily that their father was coming home, grew up with their faith shattered because he never did, and neither serves the Lord today.

Honesty with your children is so important. I don't know for sure but I wonder if things might have been different for my friend's children if she had confessed, "I married your father out of the will of God and although I know that God hates divorce, He will not force your father to do what is right. We are going to accept God's will and build our lives in Jesus Christ." Instead, years were lost waiting for a promise that existed only in her mind. Young lives were wasted and are gone.

It was certainly not wrong for Ann to hope to repair her marriage. It is true that God hates divorce, but God will not usually take away the consequences of wrong choices. The best thing to do is admit our mistakes of the past and ask Him to help us build a future. We cannot attempt to validate our wrong choices by asking God to provide an ending to the story that would make everything look all right. The only thing that matters is that He is glorified, and only He knows the path that is best. We must never forget that all the manipulations in the world cannot change the mind of God. We can certainly try to manipulate events and often do, with disastrous results. There is only one thing to do and that is to give up control and throw ourselves upon His mercy. When we wait for divine intervention, we don't have to worry about the results. God's solutions are always best and often surprising. He rarely does things the way we had planned for Him to do them but comes up with answers to our dilemmas that we never even dreamed of—more than we could ask or think—if we wait and take our hands off the situation.

So many things happen in life that we would not choose, but in not choosing the hard path we would miss some of the greatest blessings God has for us. Left alone, mankind will almost always choose the easiest road. I suppose that is why God, in His infinite wisdom, does not usually let us pick our own trials. I would choose something I know I can deal with while He will choose something to develop my character. We are good at praying qualifying prayers. I have often found myself praying, "Lord, you can do anything but this" or "I can take anything but that. . . ." Still trying to pick and choose! We have been afraid to pray, "Lord, do whatever it takes to save my loved one" or "Do what it takes to crush my will so I can be more like you." We are afraid to pray those prayers because we don't trust God. We can't quite believe the Scripture that says He will not put on us more than we can bear. But we must stand on that promise and believe that He knows exactly what it will take to answer our prayer and we must trust His will is best. Sometimes it seems answers to our prayers come easily and everything is wonderful, while at other times the price for seeing our prayers answered is painful and requires unexpected sacrifice. We can be assured that God does not answer a prayer in a way that causes pain because He enjoys seeing us suffer; rather, He does all things well and in a way that will bring ultimate glory to Him.

The first real tragedy to touch my life was the death of my oldest brother, David, who was drowned in the sinking of the world's largest offshore oil drilling platform, the *Ocean Ranger*, on February 15, 1982. He was twenty-five years old, a young husband, and the father of two. At the time, I thought nothing worse could ever happen. Our family was totally devastated and crushed. But I have lived long enough and seen enough to thank God that my brother is safe with Him. Our families visited together only eight weeks prior to his death. I did not realize it at the time but God gave me a wonderful gift, for while I was there I saw David's dedication to the small home missions church his family attended. I found out whenever he was home on Sunday, he would go to church at least an hour early so he could vacuum, straighten the songbooks, and spend quiet time with the Lord.

Now the home missions church is gone, the pastor

has left truth, but my brother is safely deposited in heaven. It is certainly not what we would have chosen, but it is what God chose in His wisdom.

> *The righteous perisheth, and no man layeth it to heart: and merciful men are taken away, none considering that the righteous is taken away from the evil to come* (Isaiah 57:1).

My parents were living in Egypt when David died, and we traveled to New Orleans to meet them as they got off the plane about forty-eight hours after the accident. Of course we were crying and devastated, but I have never forgotten my mother's first words to me, "I have never asked the Lord for anything for you kids except that you be saved. I haven't asked for good jobs or financial blessing—just that you be saved." She did not know the price she would pay for that prayer, but she accepted it.

True surrender comes when we stop trying to choose our trials and give control to the Master. That is when we can pray, "I do not know how Your will is going to be accomplished. I trust Your wisdom and only ask for strength to walk in the path You have chosen for me."

His Plan for Me

Sometimes the path He chose for me
Has led through pleasant ways,
Through peaceful valleys, quiet streams,
With warm and sunny days.
Sometimes the climb is steep and rough
With darkness overhead,
With chilling winds and falling stones,
But still the path I tread.
I know this path was planned for me
According to His will;
I've trusted Him throughout the past
And I will trust Him still.
And some day He'll reveal to me
The wisdom of His choice,
Then I'll know why this path was best
And praise Him, and rejoice.

Jewish Prayer
– Author Unknown

7
Finding Me

CHAPTER 7

Everyone carries a mental image of herself in the back of her mind that can often have little to do with reality. As James said, we see ourselves in the mirror when we get ready for the day and immediately forget what it was we saw.

> *For if any be a hearer of the word, and not a doer, he is like unto a man beholding his natural face in a glass: For he beholdeth himself, and goeth his way, and straightway forgetteth what manner of man he was* (James 1:23, 24).

Since we cannot carry a mirror with us throughout the day (people would start to think we're slightly strange), it is easy for our self-image to become distorted. There are those who think they are great beauties because they forgot what was in the mirror, and there are those who think they are ugly for the same reason.

The mature person will focus less on the outward image and more on the inner person she strives to be.

However, often without realizing it, individuals can become overly concerned with the public persona. They realize that how they are perceived as a person will largely cement their image in the minds of other people. Then comes the temptation to put up a facade. Since the coming of age of mass media, politicians are often more worried about their image and legacy than serving their electorate. Becoming obsessed with image can lead to a dichotomy in behavior—where there is one standard for the public person and another for the private person. As Christians, our behavior should have only one gold standard, and that is to please the Lord in everything we do, publicly and privately.

Jesus said, "Verily I say unto you, Except ye be converted, and become as little children, ye shall not enter into the kingdom of heaven" (Matthew 18:3). It is very enlightening to watch five- and six-year-olds interact in play. Most have no image problem at all. They think they can run faster, jump higher, and be greater than anyone else in the world. My husband, Brian, jumped off the roof of his house when he was eight years old because he was convinced he was Superman. Fortunately, he was not hurt, but he quickly learned he was not Superman. Every child reared in a loving and secure home is convinced that his life is the best, his dad is the strongest man on the block, and his mom is the prettiest woman. Only as we age and observe those around us do we begin to be shaped by peer pressure and expectations of others.

Ruth Bell Graham said, "You can experience pressure when you start thinking about those who are watching you—your kids—those you work with—relatives, fellow churchgoers—and if you think about it too much you can start to behave in ways that you think will meet others' expectations—a sure path to burnout. The only way to be the right kind of example without feeling the pressure is to be real."

Okay, God, I will be real. I want to be "the real me," but who am I? Am I a Martha or a Mary? Who do I want people *thinking* I am? There is often a contradiction between who we want people to think we are and the real person inside. We have goals and we know what we *ought* to be, but often it seems as though everyone else has it all together and we are just pretending. We have a cookie-cutter image of what a real Christian lady should be like but are having trouble fitting into that design.

Maybe you feel like Charlie Brown from the Peanuts cartoon. Lucy is telling Charlie Brown, "Life is like a deck chair. Some place it to see where they're going, others to see where they've been. Some place it to see where they are at present."

Charlie Brown replied, "I can't even get mine unfolded."

One of our deepest fears is that someone will be watching while we try to get our "deck chair" unfolded and will discover we don't have everything as together as we would have everyone think. Why do we worry about all this stuff? It seems silly but it is a very real pressure—the need to be who I am balanced against the expectations of others. Some choose conformity as a defense mechanism so they will never stand out and be noticed while others go the other way completely, choosing to be as eccentric as possible in an effort to be noticed. They want to convince people they are not average. Both groups are focused on the wrong thing— what others think. The only way to get off this merry-go-round is to focus on God's opinion. The only right way is the way that pleases Him.

It takes maturity and an understanding of how special you are to God to find peace and acceptance deep within. This is not a license to be sloppy or un-Christian. In fact, learning to look at yourself as God sees you will produce a desire to improve, without feeling condemnation that you have not already "arrived." The person who accepts bad qualities such as anger, criticism, scornfulness, and impatience as "just my personality" is not accepting her responsibility to become Christ-like. Maturity in Jesus Christ means that you accept the fact that those qualities are part of the base nature of man but can be controlled by the Holy Spirit working in you.

Honesty about self is the only true path to acceptance. If you are trying to squeeze into a mold to meet the expectations of others, you are not being honest with yourself or them. It may not be pleasant, but facing your limitations and embracing your areas of gifting will set you free from trying to meet others' expectations.

For years I tried to squeeze myself into the musician mold because that is what I thought was expected of the Pentecostal evangelist's wife. I have a very modest degree of musical talent, painfully learned over years of practice. I am not a natural musician. Some who play the keyboard only have to think of what they want to play and it seems to ooze from their fingertips. Not me. It had to translate from my brain, to paper, and then to the keyboard. Therefore, if someone switched keys, or wanted to sing a new song, it became panic time—not at all conducive to worship. When it was going well, I loved to play, but when it was going badly, I wanted to crawl into the organ bench. Ironically, very few people seemed aware of my musical limitations. Either they were being polite or I faked it very well. But I knew. I knew it panicked me and limited my worship, so I made the decision one day to stop. I found worship is a whole lot easier if I'm not thinking about which chord progression is supposed to come next. The world did not end and I am still a preacher's wife.

Without the right perspective even the most well-meaning person can fall into the trap of seeking an image rather than being true to oneself. The scale on which we weigh our image must be true and balanced. Too much attention to the opinions of others can weight it in the wrong direction. Too much stubborn-ness in having our own way and walking in our own path can weight it as well. We must all come to a point in life where we are still and can ask God to weigh us in His balance. This is when you invite Him into your private place and ask Him to expose your inner self. It is vital to do this, for if left to ourselves we will seek the path of least resistance. Most of the time our scales will be weighted by our experiences or our circum-stances and we will be easier on ourselves than we should be. That is why we *must* ask the Lord to help us.

The heart is deceitful above all things, and desperately wicked: who can know it? (Jeremiah 17: 9).

Only God truly knows, and He will reveal our motives, weaknesses, and strengths if we ask. People who insist they know their heart and proclaim their motives are always absolutely right, but are not obeying the Word of God, are in a dangerous place. We can so easily deceive ourselves. It takes an almighty, omniscient God to search our hearts, and He will always use His Word as a mirror. It is propped up in view every time we hear the Word, but we choose whether to look in it or not. In most hospitals, delivery tables are equipped with a mirror so that a mother, laboring to deliver her child, can observe the baby being born. I always chose not to look because that would definitely be in the category of things I could live my life without seeing. I knew there was a competent doctor and team of nurses to make sure everything went right. But we cannot afford to make that choice with our souls. We must be willing to look into the mirror every time the Word is preached and every time we read it.

Shall not God search this out? for he knoweth the secrets of the heart (Psalm 44:21).

C. H. Spurgeon said, "It is the easiest thing in the world to give a lenient verdict when one's self is to be tried. Be just to all, but be rigorous to yourself."[4] There are few things sadder than someone who is deluded about herself. A woman who refuses to accept advancing age and continues to dress as though she is seventeen becomes a sad caricature. People who refuse to consider they could ever be wrong, like Haman, plot the destruction of others and build their own gallows. Those who do not allow the Word to examine them walk a road of delusion, which clouds their ability to judge themselves fairly. How ironic that it is this type of person who is usually the most judgmental.

Matthew 7:2-5 should caution us of the danger of judging our own selves lightly and judging others harshly.

> *For with what judgment ye judge, ye shall be judged: and with what measure ye mete, it shall be measured to you again. And why beholdest thou the mote that is in thy brother's eye, but considerest not the beam that is in thine own eye? Or how wilt thou say to thy brother, Let me pull out the mote out of thine eye; and, behold, a beam is in thine own eye? Thou hypocrite, first cast out the beam out of thine own eye; and then shalt thou see clearly to cast out the mote out of thy brother's eye* (Matthew 7:2-5).

Those who are the most loudly judgmental often have a whole two-by-four sticking out of their own eyes which is readily apparent to those around them, yet they can always find a justification for their problem.

Some try to avoid the risk and pain involved in examining their heart by comparing themselves with others, a sure sign of immaturity. Think of the child who always says, "Well, Susie does it." To which all wise mothers respond, "Just because Susie does it does not make it right."

> *For we dare not make ourselves of the number, or compare ourselves with some that commend themselves: but they measuring themselves by themselves, and comparing themselves among themselves, are not wise* (II Corinthians 10:12).

Comparison is guaranteed to produce a twisted perspective because there will always be someone who looks better and has more talents than you, causing despair. On the other hand, there will almost always be an area in which you excel, possibly giving you a reason to be proud. This is akin to trying to produce a straight line without a plumb line or a ruler.

Comparing yourself to others is dangerous unless the one to which you are comparing yourself is perfect. There is only one who fulfills that requirement and that is Jesus Christ. Holding His Word up as the only standard by which to measure ourselves will produce purity in the inner man, and building what is on the inside will produce a far more lasting legacy than building an outward image. Paul prayed that we would be strengthened in the inner man.

> *That he would grant you, according to the riches of his glory, to be strengthened with*

might by his Spirit in the inner man (Ephesians 3:16).

It is a particularly sad sight to see an elderly person whose inner man has not grown as the outer shell deteriorates. A shell of a man or woman with a shell of a soul is not a pleasant person to be around. Their souls have shrunk along with their bodies, and their lips are full of complaints and bitterness. But some of the most fascinating people to talk to are the elderly who have rich inner lives, along with their memories. Though their bodies are broken down, they can talk for hours about the goodness of God, relating stories of His faithfulness through the years. Their stories bring hope and faith because they want you to know that if God came through for them, He will come through for you. There is no ornate facade or beauty to be seen, but they are beautiful nonetheless because of what is reflected from the mirror of their soul. It lets me know that in the end, image means nothing. It really does not matter what people have thought of them in life's journey. All that matters now is that they have ended their journey well.

Arsenic, Anyone?

CHAPTER 8

In this age of reality TV, society is shallower than ever. Time magazine recently published an article detailing how the so-called reality television shows are manipulated to provide the outcome the producers and viewers want rather than what is really happening.[5] It would be comical if it were not so indicative of the day in which we live. Reality is less important than perception. Honesty is irrelevant. Although I have never watched a reality television show and never plan to, it saddens me that our society has sunk so low.

Living in the twenty-first century is a very visual experience. Just one hundred years ago, there was no television, movies were black and white, and color photography was in its infancy. In this century we are inundated with images on every possible surface, from magazines to billboards. Worse, there is no guarantee of privacy in any public place. Someone could be taking your picture with their cell phone and you may never know. Popular magazines such as *People* and *Star* provide lurid shots of more than we want to see about celebrities. Movie stars, athletes, and music artists are the idols of the day.

Our families are constantly bombarded with these images even though we try to shield them. Society would have our children think that looking good at any price is the ultimate goal of life. Peer pressure to dress and act in a way that cheapens our daughters is very powerful. Christian values and modest dress are quickly going the way of the dinosaur. Women are encouraged to go through any kind of torture to measure up to an ideal that is almost unattainable and, at best, illusory.

It used to be that what you saw was what was real. You did not believe some things until you saw them. That no longer holds true. Hollywood has perfected special effects technology so well that even the most fantastic images can be made to look convincingly authentic. Computer programs can be used to touch up photographs and even put subjects into a shot who were not present when the photo was taken. How ironic that though we know we live in a world where almost anything can be faked and we know that what we are looking at cannot be real, we can still find ourselves reaching for the imaginary ideal.

Stores like Gap, Express, Abercrombie & Fitch, and Victoria's Secret present images of skeletal and haunted-looking models for our young people to emulate. Many women do not understand that Victoria's secret is that she has been digitally stretched and enhanced for the models to look the way they do, along with surgical enhancement in most cases. Only a select few can ever attain the standard set for beauty, yet the agenda is hammered into us day in and day out. If you look at fashion magazines, it is hard to find a model bigger than a size six, yet the average American woman wears a size fourteen. A model who wears a size twelve is considered a plus size! It is no wonder so many actors and models turn to alcohol, drugs, and other destructive behavior. Most find it hard to retain their skeletal bodies without substance abuse.

Although technology has changed, the agenda of Satan has not. Since his ejection from heaven, he has been in the business of wanting to destroy mankind, and vanity has always been one of his tools. In the eighteenth and nineteenth centuries, it was fashionable to use arsenic as a powder to make the complexion very white. Victorian women ate arsenic mixed with vinegar and chalk to keep their skin pale so people would not think they worked in the fields.[6] A natural antibiotic, arsenic also helped keep the complexion clear. The green dye derived from arsenic was used in wallpapers and even in clothing. It is now thought that some people died slowly of arsenic poisoning because the dyes would give off a gas, causing the poison to build up in the system.

It was also discovered that a pinch of arsenic worked like a tonic, giving the subject a "blooming complexion and a brilliant eye." Through trial and error they learned to take the poison for two weeks and then stop for two weeks to let it work out of the system. Sometimes people would take too much and kill themselves unintentionally. A doctor discussing the pros and cons of taking arsenic in 1856 said, "If any of your readers still feel disposed to try it they should make some written memorandum that they have done so, lest, in case of accident, some of their friends may be hanged in mistake."[7]

It is so tempting to take a little of the world's poison in order to look more like them, but a little poison is never enough. Every day its cruel voices will tell you that you are not pretty enough, sexy enough, thin enough, or smart enough. Even among Spirit-filled women, the pressure is real and it is powerful. The only way to combat it is with the Word of God and to worship at the feet of Jesus as often as possible. Although we should definitely stay informed about world events, the visual cues of the media are not designed to influence a godly standard of dress. As surely as eating too much sugar and not enough protein will start to show in your body, a steady diet of ungodly music, movies, and entertainment will show in your spirit.

Ironically, in an age where obesity is on the rise worldwide, Americans still worship thinness. Anorexia, a disorder unheard of one hundred years ago, is rampant among teens, and even adults, today. Anorexia, bulimia, and other eating disorders are affecting children as young as eight or nine because of the constant bombardment of media in their lives, where the girl who "has it all" is smart, sassy, and skeletal. We have to come to terms with our flesh and realize that five or ten extra pounds on the scale do not change us in the eyes of God. We cannot let the world's values dictate how we feel about ourselves. Conversely, we cannot use the same barometer as permission to let ourselves go. Good hygiene and grooming help us be good ambassadors for Christ. Exercise and a sensible diet keep us healthy so that we are able to fulfill the call of God.

Even those who get beyond comparing themselves to others and to the standards of the world can still be dissatisfied with the Master's design. If your hair is curly, you want it straight. If you are tall, you want to be short. If you are short, you really want to be tall. Many women I know carry on negative self-talk all the time, "I'm too hippy, too fat, too skinny, too old, too tired, too sick, too busy, too stupid, too loud, too carnal, and too lethargic to do anything about it." And before they know it, years have passed in a haze of discontent. This is not the will of God! It is not His will that you simply exist. The years go quickly and we do not have the time to waste. Before you know it, you will be looking in the mirror, facing a whole new crisis—aging.

The Prison of Vanity

CHAPTER 9

Favour is deceitful, and beauty is vain: but a woman that feareth the LORD, she shall be praised (Proverbs 31:30).

Vanity: *vanus,* empty, vain
1 : something that is vain, empty, or valueless
2 : the quality or fact of being vain
3 : inflated pride in oneself or one's appearance
Merriam-Webster Dictionary

I am sure there were vain women even in the time when Jesus walked the earth. After all, we were created with a natural desire to be attractive. You do not usually have to prompt a little girl to be "prissy." They are just born that way. Our granddaughter, Kinsey, at the age of two, is currently going through a phase where she walks around the house all day, every day in plastic high heels from Wal-Mart. She has five pairs and she puts them on the minute she wakes up and changes them during the day. She is the only two-year-old I know who can run in high heels. When it's time to go somewhere, she immediately runs for a purse and a hat. She is absolutely adorable and completely feminine.

The desire to be attractive is not inherently a bad quality and we should not confuse femininity with vanity. Our femininity is a gift from God. He made us male and female and expects a difference in behavior and dress to distinguish us from one another. Beauty is God given and there are many instances of women in the Bible who were praised for it. Both Abraham and Isaac had such beautiful wives that they sinned and lied about their relationship with them, saying they were their sisters instead of their wives.

Abigail and Esther are my personal favorites, for not only were they beautiful; they were also wise. Abigail urged David not to sin by killing her brutish husband even though she was held captive by his coarseness (I Samuel 25). Because of this she saved David's reputation and, soon after, became the wife of a king. Esther was not too beautiful to listen to the wise counsel of her cousin, Mordecai, and was able to save her entire people. These women did not let their beauty make them proud or haughty.

As a jewel of gold in a swine's snout, so is a fair woman which is without discretion (Proverbs 11:22).

Strong's Concordance describes "discretion" as perception, intelligence, taste, and understanding. A truly beautiful woman is not necessarily one with the right looks, but one who understands from where beauty comes. I have seen many a gorgeous woman whose haughty attitude makes her ugly and unpleasant to deal with, and I have also seen many women who might be considered plainer but whose beautiful spirit makes them more attractive the longer you are in their presence. These are the women who have followed the command of Peter.

> *Whose adorning let it not be that outward adorning of plaiting the hair, and of wearing of gold, or of putting on of apparel; But let it be the hidden man of the heart, in that which is not corruptible, even the ornament of a meek and quiet spirit, which is in the sight of God of great price* (I Peter 3:3, 4).

It is all about balance again. We must balance our desire for beauty against the hidden man of the heart. We certainly want the world to know that we are valued women of God. A slovenly look and unkempt hair will not convey any beauty, no matter how wonderful the state of our hearts. Proverbs 31 describes the virtuous woman as one who dresses in silk and purple. Obviously, she dressed well yet still took care that all her other duties were met. Her family was clothed and her household in order. Yet it is unprofitable to get so fixated on having every hair perfect that it becomes a big deal when something goes wrong. We women will say to each other, "It's a bad hair day," and that says it all. It becomes an excuse for being late to church, being grumpy, and generally having a bad attitude. When that happens, you can be assured your priorities are in the wrong place.

Years ago I went to a conference with another young minister's wife. We drove all day to get there and then rushed around to get ready. My hair just did not look right to me, so I insisted on taking it down and styling it again. When I finished she looked at me and said, "It looks exactly like it did before." I realized then that I had wasted time and effort for something intangible. Overemphasis on self is a time waster, especially when you finally realize that no one is noticing anyway.

An eternal perspective helps us to prioritize and realize what is really important. When Mary anointed Jesus' feet and dried them with her hair, she was focused only on worshiping Him. Those who observed her thought she was crazy or misguided. The custom of the day was probably to keep the hair bound or covered, but she did not let convention stop her. She realized that she needed to seize that moment to worship Jesus. Though we know little else about her, that act of worship has been remembered through the ages, just as Jesus said it would. When beauty has faded, only what has been done for Christ will stand.

An eternal perspective will also guide us through the rough waters of aging. We live in a society that worships youth and beauty while discarding the elderly. A youthful appearance is pursued at any cost. Sitting in an airport or mall is a fascinating exercise because you can see the search for lost youth so clearly and plaintively in the faces of seventy-year-olds with bright red hair, dressed in skin-tight jeans or short shorts. Vanity is cruel and its price is dignity.

I admit it is not fun to age. I grayed earlier than most, and I found out that people stop looking at your face. They glance up, see the gray hair, and immediately give you the senior discount! At first it upset me and I was tempted (only briefly) to stop shopping on Mondays and Tuesdays because they are senior days somewhere. Then I started noticing that the cashiers who gave me the senior discount were barely out of diapers, and that made me feel better. I remember how old someone in her forties seemed to me when I was a teenager. I have noticed lately that I am usually the only gray-haired person in the whole mall or in the airport unless I meet another Apostolic. But I refuse the chain of hair color. It is a weight and a burden (financial and otherwise) that I do not need if I am going to be the person God wants me to be. After all, that real person has gray hair.

Although we will have more peace in our hearts if we accept aging gracefully, it does not mean we should not do our best to take care of the body God has given us. An active, healthy lifestyle is the best tonic for aging. A good sunscreen is the best possible tool to keep your skin looking young. Slather it on every day, and your skin will thank you later with a minimum of wrinkles and sun damage. Remember, God made your skin to go with your hair, and as you age, your skin color changes. The seventy-year-old with dyed hair often looks strange because her skin no longer matches her hair. There is such freedom in accepting yourself as you are and enjoying the later years of life. I could go crazy looking at pictures of myself when I was nineteen years old and comparing them to pictures of myself now at (never mind). The most talented plastic surgeon in the world would not be able to make me look nineteen again. He could make me look weird—just not nineteen. I visited a dermatologist recently who tried to talk me into letting him inject Botox[8] into my forehead to "take care of" the little frown line between my eyes. I thought about it briefly until it occurred to me that his staring look was because he was so Botoxed he could barely blink! So I politely declined because I earned that wrinkle and all the others that will come.

A woman with daughters should always remember what her actions say to them. "Do what I say and not what I do" is not a rule that can be applied. Your daughters will imitate your behavior and take it even further. An overemphasis on beauty, thinness, and designer clothing will typically cause one of two reactions: she will go the other way altogether and shun any trappings of beauty, or she will become dangerously obsessed. Teaching her to shop wisely and get value for her money instead of going straight to the designer labels will serve her well. I am all for quality clothing, but I like it a whole lot better on the sale rack. Almost all young wives need to be thrifty as they start their married life, and one who is used to wearing only certain brands may have a difficult time staying in the family budget.

It seems I might have taught my girls this too well.

One day while visiting Chicago we went "shopping" on the Magnificent Mile. I use the word shopping loosely—we were looking. There was not even a shoelace we could afford, but we bravely tromped from boutique to boutique, whispering about the prices and trying to look sophisticated. We went into a shoe store where the cheapest pair was $350 and pretended to browse. The salespeople stared at us, and finally one approached Dana, who was about thirteen at the time. She complimented the shoes Dana was wearing and Dana said, "Thanks. I got them at Shoe Carnival for four dollars and they look just as good as these." The look of astonishment on their faces was priceless, and we could not get out of that shop fast enough. I'm sure the poor salesladies saw us fall on each other laughing when we got outside. We were not making fun but just enjoying the fact that we could be happy with four-dollar shoes.

Vanity is not only about looks; it is placing importance in things that have no lasting value. It can be clothing, houses, cars, and status. We must carefully teach our children that self-worth does not come from appearance or things but in having a right relationship with Jesus Christ. That is a far greater legacy to leave than all the designer clothing money can buy.

Her children arise up, and call her blessed; her husband also, and he praiseth her. Many daughters have done virtuously, but thou excellest them all (Proverbs 31:28, 29).

There's a Lizard in My Living Room

CHAPTER 10

I'm feeling pretty proud of myself today. While dust-mopping my wood floor, I thought I saw the green design moving on the area rug. It took me about two seconds to realize the design was not moving and my eyes were okay. It was a lizard. I am proud of myself because I did not call the fire department or pest control. I did not call my husband to come home from the church to get the lizard (which I confess to having done in the past). I have to admit that I yelled for Lee, our son, who was upstairs getting dressed and apparently could not hear me.

So it was me and Mr. Lizard. He ran under the couch and I thought he was lost forever. I continued into the dining room and foyer, sweeping, contemplating life with a lizard in the living room. There was no way I could sit on the couch or the love seat because they were on the side of the room where he was sitting. Maybe I would be able to sit in one of the chairs since they were on the opposite side of the room. Playing the piano would be out of the question; my back would be to him. Then a terrible thought occurred to me. I realized the living room adjoined the master bedroom and my side of the bed was nearest the door. However would I sleep, knowing there was a lizard in the living room? Maybe Brian would swap sides with me.

I had decided to be an adult about this and thought maybe I could manage life with a member of the reptile family in the house when Lee came downstairs, got the mop, and gently coaxed the lizard, which had obligingly walked out from under the couch, out the door.

He said, "I've gotten lots of lizards out of this living room, Mom."

Oh great! My family has been hiding the fact there is an occasional lizard in the house because they know I fear them. I have always loved front porches, and when we moved to Florida, God led us to the perfect home with a beautiful, white front porch that stretches almost the full length of the house. It has pretty hanging baskets and wicker chairs. It gets a full dose of the afternoon sun and would be perfect except for one thing: Florida has lizards, lizards like sunshine, and I don't like lizards. So I have to confess I never sit on my front porch. It is really quite pathetic of me, I know.

Yet how often our lives are ruled by fear. Some are healthy and God given for the survival of mankind. It is natural to be afraid of a grizzly bear because you are prey to him. Few of us, however, ever have to worry about meeting with a grizzly. Our fears are more mundane and largely irrational, yet if we are not careful we can find ourselves giving in to them. How silly it would be to lose the use of a whole room because of a tiny animal no more than four inches long that cares for humans even less than we care for them. But I was having to do some pretty serious negotiating with myself when it seemed I was going to have to live with that lizard in the house. (I am still negotiating about the porch.)

Dealing with insects, rodents, or lizards are minor examples, but we can lose out on some of life's greatest experiences because of fear's intimidation. I know a woman who is afraid to drive across a bridge. Because of this she cannot visit her children and grandchildren on her own. Some people are afraid of flying. Being a "white knuckle" flyer myself, I can relate, but my desire to go places and see things has overruled that fear. If I had let the fear of flying rule my actions I would have missed seeing the Eiffel Tower, Notre Dame, Westminster Abbey, the Tower of London, and experiencing a safari in Africa, among many other things.

Brian and I accompanied a group of young people on a Youth on Mission trip to Russia during the time when Aeroflot was still the national airline. They seemed to crash every other week, and as we all got on a flight to Orenberg, in the interior of Russia, we were terrified. But we knew we had work to do in Orenberg, so we all got on the plane in spite of our fear, along with four dogs and numerous smelly people. Once we arrived safely, the team visited hospitals and nursing homes, conducted street services, and had church services at night. The hunger of the people was evident, and as I saw the young people minister I knew none of this would have been accomplished if we had given in to fear. I thank God for every missionary, home and foreign, who has gone into a strange environment, facing the unknown and giving up comforts, to build a work for the Lord.

Here at home, we can find it risky to try something new: to speak or sing in public, to step into a new job, or to go back to school after a long absence. All these things are scary and entail risk, but I have noticed those who don't risk much miss a whole lot of new and wonderful experiences. Staying in familiar territory is safe and comforting, and exceedingly boring.

Sometimes we mask our fear in shyness, but it is worth examining ourselves to see if what we call shyness is really pride. We are afraid of failing. We don't want to look bad so we never step out on a limb. We may fear that if we really worship the Lord like we would like to in our hearts, someone will notice us. We are embarrassed. But what is embarrassment but pride? It is caring too much what someone else will think.

I have seen extreme stubbornness masked in shyness, where the person is really not afraid of what others think but is so quietly convinced that their way is the right way that they will not consider other points of view or ever try new experiences. Some are bound by family tradition and feel it would be a betrayal of their way of doing things to ever change. This, too, is a form of pride.

It appears from Proverbs 11:2 that without pride there would be no shame, "When pride cometh, then cometh shame: but with the lowly is wisdom." A proud person is not teachable. Only with humility can you gain wisdom. Conquering pride in our lives takes care of a lot of the problems we face and removes at least one source of anxiety. It is not wise to become defensive when someone does something better than you. Wisdom is teachable and takes the opportunity to learn how to do things better when confronted with excellence. Instead of scorning someone's good works, a wonderful program that is bringing results or favorite dish that everyone raves about, we should ask them for their recipe or formula for success. You will bless them by asking and you will be blessed if they share their techniques with you.

One of the fears that people face today is much more nebulous. My husband calls it the "No Name Giant." It can't really be defined but is a nameless and very real fear that something is going to go wrong. We know we are not worthy of the blessings of the Lord and fear the proverbial rug is going to be pulled out from under us any minute. This fear originates from the very heart of the enemy. Satan wants us to doubt God. If he can throw darts of fear at us and make us afraid, we are doubting God. We are afraid, whether we acknowledge it or not, that He is not willing or able to sustain us.

Many people, particularly women, live with at least a moderate level of anxiety. It is easy to become anxious over our family, friends, finances, and health. If not managed, anxiety can easily spin out of control, making our lives miserable, as well as the lives of those around us. Circumstances will always have a way of adding to the misery, seeming to conspire to drive us over the edge! While not wanting to condemn those who choose to use medication to help control their anxiety, I would like to prescribe the only true remedy:

> *Do not be anxious about anything, but in everything, by prayer and petition, with thanksgiving, present your requests to God. And the peace of God, which transcends all understanding, will guard your hearts and your minds in Christ Jesus* (Philippians 4:6-7, NIV).

It is a fact that millions of mood-altering drug prescriptions are written each year in America. Every physician you visit, from the family physician to the gynecologist, is likely to offer pharmaceutical help. Need help to relax? Try some Valium. Are you anxious? Prozac will help. Trouble sleeping? Ambien or Lunesta will take care of that. Rather than pay attention to the root cause of the problem, our culture has been programmed to reach for the medication first.

Most physicians will tell you that emotional problems and mental illness are often the result of chemical imbalances in the brain. There is some dispute regarding this theory, however. In *Anatomy of an Epidemic: Psychiatric Drugs and the Astonishing Rise of Mental Illness in America*, Robert Whitaker points out that the rate of disabling mental illness has grown from three in one thousand a century ago to twenty in one thousand presently. He points out that if any other "disease" rate had risen so drastically, it would be considered an epidemic. A growing number of physicians agree that mental illness is being *caused* by psychotropic drugs rather than being cured by them.[9]

Dr. Joseph Glenmullen, author of *Prozac Backlash*, is among a growing group of physicians alarmed over the rising use of psychotropic drugs for the "worried well." One in every ten Americans has been on Zoloft, Prozac, or Paxil.[10] It is hard to believe that twenty-eight million Americans *really* require medication to control their anxiety. In addition, one to two million schoolchildren are taking Ritalin or another type of stimulant every day to control their behavior. The United States, the most blessed and prosperous country in the world, is undeniably the most drugged. Yet society acts as if we are backward when we tell them the reason our nation is so unhappy is because we have left the precepts of God's Word far behind. Our prosperity has not brought happiness. True happiness is nowhere to be found without the presence of God in our lives.

Those who do take medication should not feel judged or condemned. Like cancer patients who require chemotherapy, or diabetics who take insulin to stabilize blood sugar, some mentally ill people require daily medication. I have a brother with bipolar disorder who would probably not be alive today if he were not on medication. He is now a fully functioning, successful businessman, husband, and father. Some who suffer from chemical depression are Spirit-filled, faithful people. Unless you are a physician, it is unfair to make judgments about who should be on medication and who should not. Starting or stopping medication is a very personal decision best left to the individual, their doctor, their pastor, and God. Indeed, pastors must be extremely careful in dispensing advice about this matter, since to do so can make them vulnerable to lawsuits.

My concern is for those who rush to the doctor for medication just to deal with the anxieties of life instead of going to the Great Physician first. Dr. Glenmullen recounts the case of a woman who was prescribed Zoloft for a nail-biting habit. Indeed, she stopped biting her nails while on the medication but began experiencing such severe memory lapses that she could not even drive routes familiar to her for years. The side effects of such powerful drugs are far too dangerous for such trivial matters. Giving Jesus Christ your cares causes no side effects except peace and joy. Having been in the ministry for thirty years, Brian and I have seen many, many people who are filled with anxiety because they are not doing the things they know are right. We have become convinced that a great deal of anxiety, though certainly not all, is caused by guilt. Those who insist on living life with themselves as the center instead of God as the center will never find peace.

Even for Spirit-filled Christians, living for Christ to the best of their ability, this world is a scary place. The clamor of political turmoil, acts of terrorism, and multiple natural disasters remind us there is plenty to be anxious about. Those who stand for any kind of morality are called "mean spirited." Religion has long been pushed out of our public schools, and there is a concerted attempt to push it out of the courts and all public places. Even religious holidays are under attack, but only if they are Christian. It would be a little hard to celebrate Easter without a risen Christ. How can we celebrate Christmas without the birth of the Savior? The secular world will be glad to try.

The only peace to be found is in Jesus Christ. It is very easy to panic when it seems we are surrounded by hostile forces, if we have not surrendered control to the Lord.

> *For ye have not received the spirit of bondage again to fear; but ye have received the Spirit of adoption, whereby we cry, Abba, Father* (Romans 8:15).

When we completely understand that God has adopted us and is now our daddy, we will realize that He is in control of all things. Every daddy wants to give his child the very best, and God is no exception to this rule. In fact, He made the rule.

To worry over finances is to forget God's promise that He will supply every need. He knows our needs as surely as we know the needs of our own children. I do not ever recall any of our children asking, "Where is our next meal coming from, Mom?" They trusted me to feed them. Babies don't worry over the supply source of their milk—they just reach for Mom or the bottle and expect the milk to be there. We breathe in and out hundreds of times a day, never considering the supply of oxygen will run out. So it is with God's goodness. Receiving from Him can be just as effortless if we can put aside our worries and inhibitions and reach for "Abba."

It is not the will of God that Spirit-filled women live in torment. Giving in to anxiety can literally drive one crazy. Because the Holy Spirit lives inside us we should be able to live in this admittedly scary world in peace because we know who is taking care of us and who is in charge. We have a strong and mighty God on our side.

> *Fear thou not; for I am with thee: be not dismayed; for I am thy God: I will strengthen thee; yea, I will help thee; yea, I will uphold thee with the right hand of my righteousness. Behold, all they that were incensed against thee shall be ashamed and confounded: they shall be as nothing; and they that strive with thee shall perish. Thou shalt seek them, and shalt not find them, even them that contended with thee: they that war against thee shall be as nothing, and as a thing of nought. For I the LORD thy God will hold thy right hand, saying unto thee, Fear not; I will help thee* (Isaiah 41:10-13).

11

God's Garden

CHAPTER 11

While pondering life's complicated issues one day during my morning devotion, I was struck by the following verse.

> *To appoint unto them that mourn in Zion, to give unto them beauty for ashes, the oil of joy for mourning, the garment of praise for the spirit of heaviness; that they might be called trees of righteousness, the planting of the LORD, that he might be glorified* (Isaiah 61:3).

I decided that day that I would not worry about my image or try to fix my world and everyone in it. I purposed to no longer worry what people think of me but to strive to be a tree of righteousness so the Lord could be glorified.

I'll be a tree. What a liberating concept! A tree doesn't worry about its image—it just is. You cannot make a tree. It is planted by the Creator, but then it has to build itself. Of course, we build ourselves by what we are fed and what we allow to be taken in through our root system. The tree's fertility depends on the soil, and we must remain planted in Christ in order to be fruitful.

Further study yielded many other verses likening the righteous to trees:

> *And he shall be like a tree planted by the rivers of water, that bringeth forth his fruit in his season; his leaf also shall not wither; and whatsoever he doeth shall prosper* (Psalm 1:3).

> *The righteous shall flourish like the palm tree: he shall grow like a cedar in Lebanon* (Psalm 92:12).

Using parables about trees, Jesus taught about righteousness and the fruit of the Spirit.

> *Even so every good tree bringeth forth good fruit; but a corrupt tree bringeth forth evil fruit. A good tree cannot bring forth evil fruit, neither can a corrupt tree bring forth good fruit. Every tree that bringeth not forth good fruit is hewn down, and cast into the fire. Wherefore by their fruits ye shall know them* (Matthew 7:17-20).

Trees were on my mind because Pensacola had recently been hit by Hurricane Ivan. Lifelong residents of this area have told us that they had never experienced such a storm. Pensacola and the surrounding areas sustained hundreds of millions of dollars in damage. After the initial shock, people began cleaning up and rebuilding. In many cases, structures are being rebuilt bigger and better than they were previous to the storm.

But I really miss the trees and, unlike buildings, they cannot be so quickly replaced. Seven million acres of forest were lost in Florida alone in the hurricane season of 2004.[11] As we drove around Pensacola to view the damage, what soon became apparent is that the size of the tree did not have much to do with whether or not it was felled by the storm. Huge oaks that had weathered many storms were turned on their sides, completely uprooted, while in our front yard, two little crape myrtles survived with barely a scratch.

When I asked about the oak trees I was told that though they are big and impressive, some varieties have shallow root systems. The lesson to be learned is that the trees' survival depended less on what was above the ground than what was below. The placement of the tree when the wind hit it also contributed to its survival. Our roots must be deep, planted and established in the Word of God, if we are going to survive some storms. There are times in our lives when our faith can be so shaken and the storm can be so devastating that only a deep root system, combined with trust that God knows exactly where we are planted, will bring us through when the winds of adversity blow. The thing about being a tree is that it does not choose where it is planted. The gardener does. The master Gardener plants His righteous tree in the prime location for its survival, and we can be assured that we will grow into the flourishing tree He wants us to be if we follow the precepts of His Word.

You only have to look at nature to understand that God likes variety. There are hundreds of varieties of trees, all beautiful in their own way. Each has its own unique qualities: bark, leaves, flowers, and fruit. Just as the tree or plant cannot change its nature, we should not strive to be what we are not. A plant that thrives best in the shade cannot be placed in full sun. A hot-house beauty will die at the first sign of frost. All the yearning and prayers that could possibly be offered will not turn someone into an orchid when she is supposed to be a bush. God's placement of you in His garden is not a mistake, and learning to accept that is an act of faith that will enable you to thrive. Though there are major differences among us we all require the same sustenance in order to grow.

For most of my life I have had a "brown thumb" rather than a green one. I could kill a plant faster than anyone I know. Only in recent years have I been able to sustain a few easy-to-grow houseplants. The secret is water. I found out you can hardly kill an ivy or a peace lily if you remember to water them at least a little. The peace lily will tell you when it needs water. Its leaves get droopier and droopier until they are completely limp; then about thirty minutes after watering, the leaves stand straight and tall again. It reminds me of many Christians who try to go as long as they can before getting a "drink" of God's Word and Spirit. Of course, the poor peace lily is at my mercy. It has to wait for me to remember to water it, but we can drink from the well of God's mercy any time we like. The righteous man is like a tree planted by the water. That means he should be able to stretch his roots and get a drink any time he wants to, for there is a steady supply to be tapped. Dry times can happen because we have changed our position and are no longer planted by the water, or we are just not reaching to the water supply. Sometimes we simply forget to drink. Though the Living Water is readily available we can get so busy and distracted that we let ourselves get parched, and then we find ourselves dragging the ground, all dried up and not really understanding what is going on. That is when we find ourselves like Martha, worried and upset, and that is when it is time to stop for a good, long drink.

Getting enough to drink requires a conscious decision for most people. It is popular wisdom that for maximum health the human body requires half its body weight in ounces of water each day. Most people have to think about getting that much water and devise a strategy to accomplish it. Some purchase huge bottles which they fill up in the morning and drink throughout the day. It is the same in the spirit. Getting enough water does not just happen. We must build strategies into our day and lifestyle to help us accomplish it.

Jesus said, "Blessed are they which do hunger and thirst after righteousness: for they shall be filled" (Matthew 5:6). Have you noticed that if you are extremely thirsty a drink is all you can think about? God wants us to long for a right relationship with Him—to hunger and thirst after righteousness at least as much as our bodies hunger for food and drink. The psalmist said, "As the hart panteth after the water brooks, so panteth my soul after thee, O God" (Psalm 42:1). You must *decide* to hunger and thirst after righteousness. Those who do will not be disappointed. They shall be filled. This is as certain as gravity. Though it may seem like a struggle to reach for those things on earth, when we reach heaven we are promised that we will no longer have to strive.

> *They shall hunger no more, neither thirst any more; neither shall the sun light on them, nor any heat. For the Lamb which is in the midst of the throne shall feed them, and shall lead them unto living fountains of waters: and God shall wipe away all tears from their eyes* (Revelation 7:16-17).

Besides getting the right amounts of water, plants must be fed. Of course, we are fed by the Bread of Life, the Word of God. Then fertilizer is added to the soil to enrich it. I have yet to discover a pleasant-smelling fertilizer. Unfortunately, periods of spiritual growth are usually really stinky times, but through pain and adversity, richness is added to the soil. But this only happens if we react properly to the trial. Wrong reactions will not produce the proper nutrients.

In the wilderness, trees are fertilized by the breaking down of dead leaves and branches that fall to the base of the trunk and rot. In other words, nutrients come from things that are shed by the tree. Every hard time I have faced has been an effort by God to get me to shed some things so I could grow in the spirit. It is not easy and it is not pleasant, but it is the way God designed it. What we shed from our spirit and let die will eventually become the fertilizer that causes us to grow into the fruitful person of God that He is calling us to be. We must learn to lean on God for our sustenance, knowing that He will make us beautiful trees in His garden if we will let Him.

Oh, to Be a Tree

Of all the things I've ever wanted to be,
I ask of the Lord to make me a tree.

Not a fragile flower, known for its beauty;
Not a five-star general bound by duty;

Not a princess of "Diana" fame;
Not a star whom everyone knows by name.

Just a tree, with roots deep and branches high,
Lifting praise and worship to the sky.

Give me a sturdy trunk for leaning on,
Restful shade for those burning in the sun.

May my roots grow deep, nourished by your Word
so that I may share what I have heard.

Let my wounds bring forth sap that is clear and sweet,
cleansing guile and bitterness and self-defeat.

No glamour, no glory may ever be seen
by those who follow me.

Yet the greatest thing I could ever be
is the planting of the Lord, a righteous tree.

Lanette Kinsey

The Root of Bitterness

CHAPTER 12

Follow peace with all men, and holiness, without which no man shall see the Lord: Looking diligently lest any man fail of the grace of God; lest any root of bitterness springing up trouble you, and thereby many be defiled (Hebrews 12:14-15).

Dealing with such a sobering subject as bitterness is a little scary. Many great men and women have preached and written books concerning the danger of the root of bitterness, dealing with the subject much better than I could ever hope to. Though I have no basis on which to prove my theory, it seems to me that women are more prone to this malady than men. I know, of course, that it can affect both sexes and have certainly seen it manifested in both. However, women set the tone for the atmosphere of their home. A woman who has a calm, quiet spirit will have a calm home, while the exuberant, spirited lady will have party time all the time. Whether a home is organized or chaotic depends largely on the woman (fair or not), so it seems logical to me that the enemy would try to introduce the poison of bitterness to a family through the woman. Because most women are naturally compassionate, injustice and inconsistency can really disturb them, causing wounds that lead to bitterness.

There is no doubt that wounds will come. No one can escape this life without experiencing some pain. It is the nature of human flesh that people will hurt you. People of God will hurt you, intentionally and unintentionally. No matter how nice you are, no matter how accommodating, whether you are pleasant or unpleasant, whenever you interact with people you will eventually be hurt, and no one can hurt you quite as badly as someone who knows and loves you. Family relationships and relationships formed with people in the church carry potential for hurt because we are human beings. It seems much easier to shrug off the offense of a stranger than one committed by a brother.

A brother offended is harder to be won than a strong city: and their contentions are like the bars of a castle (Proverbs 18:19).

In addition to interaction with people, circumstances in life can disappoint you and introduce a root of bitterness. We can even become offended at God when things happen that we do not understand. Offense can become a prison unless we learn to let it go. But we must be honest. It can be really hard to let go. Maybe you have wondered, as have I: What exactly is letting go, and how do I go about it?

As a child I remember being afraid of two "great sins" the preacher often referred to: blaspheming the Holy Ghost and bitterness. I found out that you cannot accidentally blaspheme the Holy Ghost. It is a willful turning away and denying of His power. But I still worried about bitterness. I wondered, "How do I know if I'm bitter? Is it wrong to hurt? Does the pain I am feeling mean I am bitter? What is the exact moment that pain turns to bitterness, and how can I avoid it?"

The Word of God contains many warnings about bitterness. It makes very clear that it is harmful and to be avoided and specifically warns against the *root* of bitterness. The roots of a tree must be protected because its survival depends on healthy roots. A tree with a healthy root system can live through a lot of damage to the leaves and bark, but once the roots are affected, it is in grave danger. A healthy tree actually manufactures and sends bad-tasting chemicals to its leaves to repel insects that are feeding on it and sends decay-resistant chemicals to a wound to give the wound or gash time to heal without further decay.[12] It does not stop the insects or disease altogether but it keeps the balance in favor of the tree. It may look a little ragged for a while but the tree will survive. When you are hurt, the leaves of your tree might wilt for a time. It is normal to feel the pain of an offense but the danger comes when we do not deal with it, allowing the poison to fester in our spirit. It can take from three to seven years for damaged roots to cause the demise of a tree. All the time it looks fine but it gets harder and harder for the tree to fight off the things that would destroy it, until finally the decay begins to show and the tree dies.

The scary fact about bitterness is that you can hardly ever get anyone to admit that it is affecting them. They feel perfectly justified in their feelings, and taken at face value, it might seem they are. Bitterness springs from legitimate and real hurt. It is easy to begin to dwell on the injustice of that hurt, and that is where the taint of bitterness begins. I doubt there is one person on this earth who will not somewhere face the potential for bitterness, so it is important that we not beat ourselves up with guilt when it begins to attack us.

As I faced a situation that could lead to bitterness I began to seek the Lord to help me escape it. I am a Martha—not Mary. Mystical talk about giving in, letting go, and letting the Spirit deal with it does not sit well with a Martha. We need practical steps. Not long after I prayed, God allowed my spiritual eyes to be opened to those who are bitter. As I sat with a dear friend and listened to the person talk about the injustice done against them years ago, I realized I had heard this all before, many, many times.

Not that which goeth into the mouth defileth a man; but that which cometh out of the mouth, this defileth a man (Matthew 15:11).

Those who are bitter can't stop talking. They reiterate the circumstance over and over, each time pumping bitterness into their own spirit. Unfortunately, it also spills over into the lives of those around them, affecting children and acquaintances.

That is when God gave me the three steps I needed to eradicate bitterness in my life. They are very simple: (1) shut up, (2) die, (3) praise.

Shut up. Very inelegant and rude but very effective. Stop talking about the wrong done to you, because each time you open your mouth you are defiling yourself and those around you. Bitterness must be cut off at the source. Realize that the wrong done to you is not the source; your tongue is. James 3:6 confirms that the tongue will do far more damage to your spirit and to the body of Christ than any hurt inflicted upon you.

> *And the tongue is a fire, a world of iniquity: so is the tongue among our members, that it defileth the whole body, and setteth on fire the course of nature; and it is set on fire of hell* (James 3:6).

Do I ever slip up? Absolutely.

Have there been times that I must talk to someone or explode? Unfortunately.

The best thing to do in this situation is to find a godly mentor or close family member who will not indulge your hurt but will listen and allow you to blow off steam without betraying your confidence. Many times I have seen people blow off steam strategically to someone they know will repeat everything that is said. This is just a better way of spreading the poison because the person they repeat it to will have a confidant they repeat it to, and before you know it, as James said, the whole body is defiled.

The second step is simple also: Die.

Die to the need to be right.

Die to the need to feel justified.

Die to the notion that the person who hurt you will miraculously change.

Die to the need for vindication. It will probably never happen and if you don't nail those expectations into a coffin and bury them, you will never be able to forgive the person and go on. Once you let the feelings and expectations die, it is amazing how free you can be to interact with the ones who hurt you.

The last step is to praise your way into victory. This is the only way to get out of the mourning phase that extreme hurt brings. It is painful to die to self and bury the feelings and offenses that have come to you. Go ahead and mourn the things you have lost; then praise God for the plans He has for your future for you can be sure He does not wish you ill. Jeremiah penned a beautiful promise from the Lord.

> *For I know the thoughts that I think toward you, saith the LORD, thoughts of peace, and not of evil, to give you an expected end* (Jeremiah 29:11).

God has a wonderful future in mind for you, and the offenses committed against you by others cannot stop it. You hold the key to breaking out of captivity.

"Then you will call upon me and come and pray to me, and I will listen to you. You will seek me and find me when you seek me with all your heart. I will be found by you," declares the LORD, "and will bring you back from captivity. I will gather you from all the nations and places where I have banished you," declares the LORD, "and will bring you back to the place from which I carried you into exile" (Jeremiah 29:12-14, NIV).

Bitterness that has taken over a life effectively sends the spirit into exile but it does not have to stay there. All it takes to escape is a willingness to seek Him with your whole heart.

When my heart was grieved and my spirit embittered, I was senseless and ignorant; I was a brute beast before you. Yet I am always with you; you hold me by my right hand. You guide me with your counsel, and afterward you will take me into glory. Whom have I in heaven but you? And earth has nothing I desire besides you. My flesh and my heart may fail, but God is the strength of my heart and my portion forever. Those who are far from you will perish; you destroy all who are unfaithful to you. But as for me, it is good to be near God. I have made the Sovereign LORD my refuge; I will tell of all your deeds (Psalm 73:21-28, NIV).

Telling of His deeds will set you free.

When Winter Comes

CHAPTER 13

The master Gardener places a new plant lovingly and carefully in the spot He prepares just for it. He knows exactly how much sunlight or how much shade it needs. He carefully fertilizes it, waters it, and tends it during the growing season. The leaves look green and glossy, the blooms are beautiful, the scent wonderful. He put you where you are because you are the perfect accent for that portion of His garden.

Then comes winter. The gardener knew it would come. He knew the leaves would fall off and the tree would appear to be dead. The gardener does not chop down the tree or dig up the plant in its dormant season, but patiently waits for spring. When you see someone who appears to be experiencing a season of winter, do not write her off. Don't be eager to run out and chop down the tree with speculation about why she is in winter. We do not question the natural seasons and feel the world is being punished because winter has arrived. We understand that even the most prolific trees shed their leaves when the time comes. Even evergreen plants experience seasons: spring and summer when they might bloom and grow taller and fuller, autumn and winter when they are dormant. God gave us the seasons so the natural cycle of life would be sustained.

> *Verily, verily, I say unto you, Except a corn of wheat fall into the ground and die, it abideth alone: but if it die, it bringeth forth much fruit* (John 12:24).

We should not automatically assume that something is wrong or sinful in the life of a Christian who is experiencing a time of winter. That is not to say that God does not send times of chastisement. However, it is never our business to judge whether the trial is chastisement or a natural cycle of life unless we are the one going through it. Usually, the person in a winter season knows immediately in her own heart if there are problems that need addressing, and the prudent thing to do is repent and get on with the process of making things right. But there are times when even the most spiritual person in the world cannot figure out what is going on. Job must have wondered what he had done to deserve the trials he went through. Even though he was a perfect man, he used the time of chastisement and trial to examine himself.

The friends who came to assist in the examination process were sadly mistaken about Job. He was going through a trial because God was using him to show Satan a perfect man. Yet we tend to automatically assume that someone else's trial is a result of sin or imperfection. The best thing is not to speculate at all but to come alongside them with nourishment and encouragement. Remember, if their roots are deep and they continue feeding from the Word of God and receiving the sunshine of the Spirit of God, they will bloom again.

Somewhere along the way it is inevitable that each of us will enter a season of winter. It does not matter whether it is self-induced, circumstantially induced, or God induced. You cannot reason with it and you cannot make it go away. You have to dig your roots in and wait till the season passes. The winter season is not always the time to ask, "What did I do?" but rather, "What can I be? What can I learn so that I will be more fruitful when spring comes?"

I have had such a blessed life. I have often marveled in the fact that I am married to a wonderful husband and have three great kids. We have all enjoyed working in the kingdom of God together. Life, while not always easy, has been the perfect story of hard work, progress, and blessing of God leading to "success."

Our oldest daughter, Lisa, had a storybook wedding in July 1998. She and her husband, Bryan Parkey, began to pastor in Poplar Bluff, Missouri, and in the normal course of events, Lisa became pregnant. We were all thrilled to find out the baby was a boy, and on September 24, 2000, Dylan Henry Parkey entered the world with great fanfare and rejoicing. The next day joy turned to ashes as a pediatric ophthalmologist sat the family down and told us that Dylan has a condition called aniridia.

Doctor Goodrich tried to be as kind as he knew how, but he was very matter of fact as he told us that aniridia, which literally means "lack of iris," is usually caused by a deletion in the PAX 6 gene. The iris (the colored part of the eye) is actually a muscle that opens and closes to regulate the amount of light coming into the eye. When the iris is missing the pupil cannot contract to block excess light, making bright sunlight and glare a real problem for aniridics. Think of going outside on an extremely bright day and how it takes your eyes a few seconds to adjust. An aniridic eye cannot compensate so people with this condition must wear sunglasses and hats to help shield the glare. Dylan's retinas are also underdeveloped, resulting in low vision.

Doctor Goodrich told us that the first order of business would be a DNA test. If there was a deletion in the gene, we could expect that Dylan would be mildly retarded, have a 400 percent greater risk of contracting Wilm's Tumor (a childhood kidney cancer) and other complications, including glaucoma, cataracts, and blindness.

My heart broke as Lisa asked the doctor if Dylan would be able to run and play ball, and he replied, "He'll be able to run but there could be some difficulty in seeing the ball."

My son-in-law very bravely and calmly said, "We will deal with whatever comes."

Winter came to my spirit with a bang. There was no gentle autumn leading to it. I was hit with a full-fledged blizzard out of the blue. There are people who have faced similar, and far worse situations, but that day I felt like my perfect world had ended. I felt betrayed. It had been in the news only two weeks prior that Michael Douglas and Catherine Zeta Jones, two movie stars who were not even married, had an infant son they named Dylan. Their baby was a perfect little boy. My daughter and her husband pastor a church, had been great kids who always loved the Lord. Neither had ever backslidden. They had always lived for God. I felt they did not deserve this.

Then I began to act like Mary. Don't you mean Martha? No. Where was Mary after Lazarus died? She was shut up in the house. Martha was the one who went out to meet Jesus.

Then Martha, as soon as she heard that Jesus was coming, went and met him: but Mary sat still in the house (John 11:20).

Some believe Mary was too devastated to come out, and I can identify with that. After all, they had been some of Jesus' best friends. Their home was always open to Him, yet He did not come in their time of need.

It is interesting to note both Martha and Mary said the same thing to Jesus. Martha said in verse 21, "Lord, if thou hadst been here, my brother had not died." When Mary finally went to meet Him after being summoned by Martha, she said exactly the same words, "Lord, if thou hadst been here, my brother had not died" (verse 32). Yet Jesus responded to each woman differently. For the take-charge Martha, he answered every statement.

> *Then said Martha unto Jesus, Lord, if thou hadst been here, my brother had not died. But I know, that even now, whatsoever thou wilt ask of God, God will give it thee. Jesus saith unto her, Thy brother shall rise again. Martha saith unto him, I know that he shall rise again in the resurrection at the last day. Jesus said unto her, I am the resurrection, and the life: he that believeth in me, though he were dead, yet shall he live: And whosoever liveth and believeth in me shall never die* (John 11:21-26).

Then he asked a question of His own, "Believest thou this?" (verse 26), giving Martha a chance to declare her faith, "Yea, Lord: I believe that thou art the Christ, the Son of God, which should come into the world" (verse 27).

There is one sure thing about a Martha. She may not always be the most demonstrative person in the world. Martha may tend to get a little ruffled, but usually she has a deep, abiding faith that ultimately will rise to the surface. She firmly believed that Jesus was the Christ, and adversity was not going to change that fact.

Jesus' response to Mary was completely different. "When Jesus therefore saw her weeping, and the Jews also weeping which came with her, he groaned in the spirit, and was troubled" (verse 33). Jesus did not rebuke Mary or ridicule her but sympathized with her feelings. As a parent, I hurt when my children hurt, yet I know there are trials they must go through in order to learn the lessons needed. Some have speculated that Jesus' groaning was impatience with the people who had seen Him resurrect the son of the widow of Nain and perform many other miracles. Some feel He was groaning over the price of sin that He would soon have to pay. We will not really know until eternity, but it makes no difference to the outcome. He did what He came to do. He did not wait for a perfect response from Martha or Mary. As a Father, He was moved with compassion and responded to their need. Sometimes we can feel perhaps God will not answer our prayer because our response has been weak or downright wrong when faced with adversity. But He is always moved with compassion as long as we reach for Him, and we can be assured that His answers are only delayed so that His perfect will can be carried out.

The resurrection of our hopes began only a few days after Dylan was born, as the General Conference of the United Pentecostal Church International was convening in Birmingham, Alabama. Bryan's family called to say that the conference had opened with prayer for Dylan. Only twenty minutes later the phone rang again, and this time it was Dr. Goodrich calling personally *at night* to tell us that Dylan's DNA test results showed no deletion! We were not educated enough about aniridia at the time to realize what the doctor was saying, but we knew he thought it was good news. Now we know that it means Dylan only has aniridia, which is still no picnic but much better than the litany of complications the doctor had told us about. His kidney cancer risk dropped to 10 percent and his mental and motor skills are normal. In fact, he is one of the sharpest little boys around.

There is no way to tell how long your winter will last, but you can be assured that it will end. The important thing is not to give up. Don't beat yourself up and say, "I should be green and bright and fruitful all the time." Don't put yourself on a guilt trip. *Just dig deeper.* Get your roots as deep as you can and hold on. Remember, we're all in different seasons at different times, and like the natural seasons, this one will pass. And keep this in mind—the tree does not change. Only its appearance does. The leaves fall and die but the tree remains. You may feel stripped, barren, hopeless, and you really don't look that good either—but you are standing, and that is the important thing. Keep standing because spring is coming.

There Is Always a Spring

CHAPTER 14

After the last frost in Florida we prune the crape myrtles. It is not enough that the poor bush has lived through winter, suffering through the cold and the loss of all its blooms. Then it has to suffer the indignity of being pruned. The first year we lived here we pruned delicately and the crape myrtles did okay, but I noticed my neighbors' pruning jobs. Nothing delicate about them. They pruned them way down till there was nothing but nubs on the branches. I could hardly believe they could even survive, much less bloom again, but they do. They bloom again and again all through the growing season if they have been cut back. The ones that are not pruned are not nearly as prolific as those that are.

I don't like it any more than you do, but unfortunately we have to accept the pruning process in order to be fruitful. If spring comes and you still have all the old dead stuff from last season cluttering your spirit, your growth will be hindered. If we want to grow we have to accept the painful process of pruning. Rick Warren, pastor of Saddleback Church, said, "There is no growth without change, there's no change without loss and there is no loss without pain."[13] We don't welcome pain, but we learn to endure so we can grow.

The easiest way to be pruned is to let the Word do it. That takes an honest look at self while asking God to help change the qualities that are less than beneficial. It is a human trait to be easy on self while being hard on others, but only brutal honesty about your own qualities will effect change. Some of us think we are flowering magnolias when we're really a cactus. If you are constantly finding yourself in the same old situation, where it seems everyone around you is always wrong and every problem is always the other person's fault, it is probably time to ask, "Is it me? What do I need to change?" Even if you are totally innocent and react in the proper way to all situations, there are always lessons to be learned in dealing with others.

Sometimes God prunes us for reasons we don't understand until one day we can step back and see the big picture. Many times Brian and I have looked back and watched the puzzle pieces fall into place as we realize, "Oh, that's why. . . ." Then we realize that accepting God's pruning times, though they were painful and we did not understand, paid off in the long run. God sees the end from the beginning, and He was saving us from future pain or setting the stage for future blessing.

There is a gap between pruning and blooming again. The plant has been cut down to almost nothing but brown, seemingly dead branches, and if we don't have faith that we will bloom again, it would be very tempting to give up. After surviving the winter blast, then being cut down to nothing by the gardener, we may think all hope is gone, but this is not the time to despair. It's the time to have hope because if the gardener is pruning you, that means He is paying attention. If you will be patient, eventually a small green shoot will appear, then another, until one day you are a fully flowering branch again. Then you can spread joy to others with the beauty of your display.

I watched this process as we dealt with Dylan's disability. While his parents were strong and optimistic, I felt stripped to the bone by despair and uncertainty and spent the first year of Dylan's life with a great deal of anxiety. As he grew it was obvious that he could not see further than three or four feet. There is no reliable way to measure visual acuity in an infant, so we could not really be sure. He wanted someone with him continually (as all babies do) and we came to realize it was because his world was so very small. But gradually, so gradually, things started to improve and I have watched as one green shoot after another began to appear. It became evident his vision was expanding.

Lisa had been able to sneak past him as long as she was very quiet, but one day she called and excitedly said, "Mom, I thought I'd sneak by into the kitchen but Dylan saw me go by and started crying." Not many people get excited when the baby starts crying, but we were thrilled! Then, "Mom, Dylan mimicked the evangelist we had today. That means he can see the platform!" Every milestone has been a celebration and an occasion to worship the Lord.

Everything is not perfect, but Dylan doesn't know the difference. His vision is about 20/100, which enables him to do anything he wants to do. He colors and builds things (constantly) and sings and plays ball and jumps and runs. He loves preaching, and he compliments his dad or his papa after every service. When they get in the car after church he'll always say, "That was a good service." He is a regular, rough-and-tumble 400-carat little boy who likes to tease his sister, Kinsey Elizabeth, born in December 2003. All he knows is that the sun is *really* bright and he has to wear sunglasses and a hat outside. And that's taught me a lot about perspective. From Dylan's perspective, all is well.

I admit to a pang of hurt when I see him hold his books close to his face to see. When Kinsey smiles at me with her huge, brilliant blue eyes, I know that is how Dylan's would be. Instead he has big black pupils. Then the enemy wants to whisper, "See? Why would God do that? He'll struggle all his life." When he swings his bat to hit the ball but rarely does unless his daddy is there to guide him, it breaks my heart. Then I realize that just as Dylan's daddy is there to cheer him on, so is my heavenly Father. God made him. God formed him. God saw him in his mother's womb and he is a very special tree in God's garden. I have seen how God has equipped him with incredibly good humor and leadership skills—qualities that are going to help him overcome any obstacle.

Just as God has equipped Dylan to be an overcomer, He has equipped each one of us to be one also. Dylan will never see normally without a miracle but I know that God has a plan for Him. I learned that if we hold on in the winter and through the pruning time, spring is wonderful. I admit it—I had a crisis of faith. In fact, it was stripped to the bone, possibly so the Lord could rebuild me, one layer at a time. I still don't understand, but I do believe! I can say with Martha, "Yea, Lord: I believe that thou art the Christ, the Son of God, which should come into the world" (John 11:27).

Lazarus was still dead when Martha said this to the Lord. She could not have known that Jesus would resurrect him. Jesus is still Lord whether Lazarus is dead or alive. The outcome does not really matter if we come to a true understanding of who Jesus is in the process. We can gain joy and peace for the rest of the journey if we come to know and worship Him, the one who is in control of it all.

It's Just Bricks

CHAPTER 15

Dylan announced to his mother recently that he wanted to move to Pensacola so he could spend the night with Poppa and Nanna. He spends the night with Grandpa and Grandma Parkey at least once a week, and he was realizing that we lived too far away for that to happen with us.

Lisa said, "Well, what about our church? What about Cornerstone Tabernacle?"

He replied, "Mom, that's just bricks. I'll come back to visit the *people* every once in a while."

Five-year-olds are extremely literal, but there was a huge amount of wisdom in Dylan's statement. Bricks mean nothing. The people are what count.

I thank God for every beautiful church building. I thank God for the home He has given us and for every blessing He has bestowed, but I thank Him most of all for relationships. He was not satisfied after creating the heaven and the earth, the fish in the sea, and the animals on land. Even God was not fulfilled until He had someone with whom to have a relationship.

Wood rots or burns, bricks can be crushed, hurricanes can destroy our homes, but relationships are forever. Our families are the only thing we can take with us to heaven. They and the souls we influence for God are our only real legacy. When God restored all that Job had lost, He replaced it with double the amount he had before: fourteen thousand sheep when he had had seven thousand, six thousand camels instead of three thousand, one thousand yoke of oxen to replace five hundred. But God did not give Job twenty children to replace the ten who had died, for those who have died are not really gone. Our children's souls will live forever somewhere.

In the end, Martha and Mary are about the same thing. They love the Lord, their families, and the people of God. They expressed it in different ways but both were unshakeable in their faith.

The final mention of Martha and Mary in Scripture again typifies their two natures.

Then Jesus six days before the passover came to Bethany, where Lazarus was which had been dead, whom he raised from the dead. There they made him a supper; and Martha served: but Lazarus was one of them that sat at the table with him. Then took Mary a pound of ointment of spikenard, very costly, and anointed the feet of Jesus, and wiped his feet with her hair: and the house was filled with the odour of the ointment (John 12:1-3).

Martha served and Mary washed the feet of Jesus. Each took what she had and gave it to Him in worship. If Mary was the younger sister, living in Martha's home, it is quite possible the ointment with which she anointed the Master's feet was all she had. No father is mentioned to pay a dowry. No husband is mentioned who could have left her a home of her own. Mary gave what she had by breaking the box and anointing the feet of Jesus. Martha gave what she had by opening her home in hospitality and serving her guests.

The Lord wants a relationship with you, the real you. He doesn't classify us into Marthas and Marys. To Him we are unique. He loves us as we are but He wants all of us. If you serve, serve with all your heart. If you play and sing, play and sing with all your might. If you preach or teach, do it for His glory. Dedicate your family to Him. Dedicate your time to Him. Dedicate every part of your life to His service.

I want Jesus to know me, and for that I must build a relationship with Him. When you are feeling flawed and hopeless, when circumstances of life seem to conspire against you, remember John 11:5, "Now Jesus loved Martha, and her sister, and Lazarus." John was perhaps Jesus' closest disciple when He walked the earth, and he knew love when he saw it. Jesus loved Martha with all her flaws. He loved her enough to chide her gently and to instruct her about choosing the better part. For that reason, I like to think she understood when Mary broke her box of ointment. As the house was filled with its odor while she served, perhaps she basked in its savor.

So while I strive for the better part, every day I like to put my name in the verse in John, "Now Jesus loved Lanette. . . ."

Put your name there and know He loves you, too. Everything else is just bricks.